Praise

What an incredible blessing ... finding your way to, or back to, that spiritual exp... your life—being and living the sanctified life! Kevin Watson skillfully writes and warmly invites the entire Wesley Family, with all its differences, uniqueness, and similarities, to experience or re-experience the one thing that binds us together as a spiritual community and spiritual descendants of John Wesley, the experience of sanctification.

—**Bishop John Mark Richardson Sr.**
California New Journey Jurisdiction, Church of God in Christ

Phrases like *entire sanctification*, *full salvation*, *holiness*, and *second blessing of holiness* reminds me of a personal call to which I respond in the affirmative. I applaud a clear call to awaken ourselves to the blessing and gift of entire sanctification and I celebrate not simply a link to a tradition of teaching but a real experience that does translate into hope and healing . . . from the uttermost to the uttermost.

—**General Brian Peddle**
The Salvation Army International, London, England, UK

Some years ago, I heard Kevin say that if we Methodists do not take the doctrine of entire sanctification seriously, we are guilty of taking up needless space in the body of Christ. This is our unique contribution to the world and perhaps now is exactly the time to champion this doctrine. The world has never been more in need of an outpouring of holy love. And how could perfect love not be the logical goal toward which all Christ-followers are headed? There is nothing in Scripture about arriving short of that goal.

—**Rev. Carolyn Moore**, DMin, Founding Pastor
Mosiac United Methodist Church, Evans, Georgia

In *Perfect Love*, Kevin Watson reclaims the centrality of this doctrine, which will deliver us simultaneously from mainline malaise as well as from generic evangelicalism, and restore this vital witness of the gospel. The genius of Watson's work is that he moves us from understanding sanctification as merely a "crisis event" to the deeper role Christian community plays in a process, including accountability bands and a necessary heightened view of our sinfulness. This book powerfully reminds us how far we have drifted from the apostolic Christianity of our origins, what Wesley called "scriptural Christianity." I believe that the message of this book needs to be heard in fresh ways across the church and I applaud Watson for yet another landmark book in rebuilding our movement.

—**Timothy C. Tennent**, PhD, President,
Asbury Theological Seminary, Wilmore, Kentucky

Perfect Love is a clarion call back to a core teaching of the Methodist movement. I moved through its pages with joy and wonder. The author reintroduces the doctrine of sanctification with brilliant clarity and great practical insight. Written to be used by anyone seeking to grow their faith in love, *Perfect Love* should become a foundational document for seminarians and Sunday school classes. This book will play a key part in the emergence of a new day for the Methodist movement alongside a rediscovery of class and band meetings.

—**Bishop Mike Lowry**, Resident Bishop of the Central Texas Conference
Fort Worth Episcopal Area, United Methodist Church

As Kevin Watson writes in *Perfect Love*, we hope with a "holy desperation" for the power of the Holy Spirit in our lives. Along with a clear description of John Wesley's understanding of holiness and practical advice on how to receive entire sanctification. Watson's book on recovering the doctrine and experience of entire sanctification is exactly what is needed for the church at this very moment.

—**Douglas M. Strong**, PhD, Dean of the School of Theology
Seattle Pacific University, Seattle, Washington

Kevin Watson's profound, practical, and passionate appeal to reclaim the formative elements of John Wesley's movement is powerfully informative and inspiring. As a part of the global Methodist family, I found myself convicted, challenged, and ultimately convinced of the importance of this call to return to our mission to "spread scriptural holiness." May we expect, and, yes, experience, perfect love.

—**Bishop W. Darin Moore**, The African Methodist Episcopal Zion Church, Mid-Atlantic District and Immediate Past Chair of the National Council of Churches, USA, Largo, Maryland

Watson's book is a timely gift for the church universal. He reintroduces the "grand depositum" of early Methodism—the audacious and optimistic teaching that Christian faith is more than forgiveness of past sins and pardon. Here we are taken back to the rich doctrine of full salvation; that is, empowerment for holy living and freedom from the clutches of sin in the here and now. This is, indeed, the reason God raised up a people called Methodist. John Wesley himself would be well-pleased with Watson's book, which sounds much like Father John himself, who consistently calls us to go higher into God's love.

—**Bill T. Arnold**, PhD, Professor of Old Testament Interpretation
Asbury Theological Seminary, Wilmore, Kentucky

With passion, clarity, and focus Kevin Watson yearns for the broad Methodist movement to experience, preach, and claim an infusion of perfect love—holiness. Watson's scholarly grounding and pastoral focus remind me of salvationist Samuel L. Brengle. I will be recommending *Perfect Love* for the rest of my life.

—**Captain Dr. Andy Miller III**, Area Commander and Pastor
The Salvation Army, Tampa, Florida

We commend Kevin Watson's latest book, *Perfect Love*, to anyone who is a serious follower of Jesus Christ and especially to those of us who are heirs of the holiness movement. But be warned, this is not a book for the faint of heart! It is hard for us to imagine anyone reading Watson's unvarnished unpacking of Wesley's doctrine of entire sanctification and its vital role in fueling our movement without a profound awareness of how far we have drifted from the moorings of this key distinctive of Methodism. We are reminded of Wesley's prediction that if future Methodists were ever to stray from the doctrine, spirit, and disciplines of the pursuit of holiness, we would become a dead sect. May the Lord of the church use this book to revive us again!

—**Bishops Linda Adams**, **Keith Cowart**, and **Matt Whitehead**
Free Methodist Church USA

This timely book is a gift to the entire Methodist family of our blessed heritage of biblical truth. It inspires believers to rediscover the what, why, and how for transformation in the image of God by the sanctifying power of the Holy Spirit. Kevin Watson, scripturally and historically, communicates the core belief of the doctrine and experience of entire sanctification. This book should be on the shelf of every Wesleyan leader and every Bible study/small group leader.

—**Dr. Nina Gunter**, General Superintendent Emerita, Church of the Nazarene

Some of us have had to answer these questions: Are you going on to perfection? Do you expect to be made perfect in love in this lifetime? More of us have prayed multiple times to the God from whom no secrets are hidden that his Holy Spirit would "cleanse the thoughts of our hearts so that we might perfectly love." All of us ought to read Kevin Watson's fine, accessible treatment on what it means to answer these questions, offer this prayer, and attend to the historical core of Wesleyanism.

—**Lester Ruth**, PhD, Research Professor of Christian Worship
Duke Divinity School, Durham, North Carolina

As I read *Perfect Love* my heart leapt within me. My imagination cannot grasp the enormous outpouring God would do in this generation and those to come if we recover entire sanctification. May it be so Lord!

—**Dr. Jo Anne Lyon**, General Superintendent Emerita
The Wesleyan Church, Fishers, Indiana

This book lit a fire in me that I hope never goes out. Kevin Watson reminded me of the unique nature of the Methodist movement and why it captivated my heart so many years ago. The book will change the way I preach and teach. It gives me hope for the future! If you are pastor, this will be the most important book you will read this year.

—**Rev. Jacob Armstrong**, Founding Pastor
Providence Church, Mt. Juliet, Tennessee

Here is a book that could redirect and change Methodism. Methodists should not be satisfied with lukewarm Christianity. Kevin Watson urges that we recommit to our historic message of entire sanctification; live our General Rules and transform the world.

—**Riley Case**, Associate Director of the Confessing Movement, Kokomo, Indiana

This is a fine book. In many ways it fills a need for a contemporary statement of Wesley's theme in *A Plain Account of Christian Perfection*. In winsome yet direct language, Watson makes the case the Christian life is not about going to heaven, but experiencing the love of God in all its fullness. This is a book for every Methodist.

—**John N. Oswalt**, PhD, Visiting Distinguished Professor of Old Testament
Asbury Theological Seminary, Wilmore, Kentucky

Perfect Love is a book that has been needed for a long time. What John Wesley gave the original Methodists in *A Plain Account of Christian Perfection* Kevin has refreshed for our generation and generations yet to be born.

—**Maxie D. Dunnam**, Executive Director, Christ Church Global,
Memphis, Tennessee

As a people called Methodist, it appears segments of our movement are waking up from decades-long theological amnesia. Our understanding of grace, and the way it was embedded in the preaching and practices of the early days of our movement, have often been adulterated or lost in recent memory. That is why I thank God for scholars like Dr. Kevin Watson. Writing in clear language and a winsome spirit, he invites us to rediscover, preach, and put perfect love (sanctifying grace) into practice. This book will help the reader to understand the reality of the truth of this doctrine, and inspire them to pursue it for themselves and others.

—**Rev. Jeffrey E. Greenway**, DMin, Senior Pastor,
Reynoldsburg United Methodist Church, Reynoldsburg, Ohio

Kevin Watson's *Perfect Love* portrays the Wesleyan doctrine of entire sanctification for what it is—the promise that we can be changed. Rather than a set of rules or a restrictive leash, Watson describes the concept of Christian perfection as God's gracious invitation to a future that is hopeful, transformative, and the deepest desire of every believer's heart.

—**Rob Renfroe**, President, Good News, The Woodlands, Texas

From the first word to the last, the Holy Spirit was stirring my soul to desire more of God's sanctifying work in our lives and through the people called Methodist. The words leapt off the page as I said out loud many times "Yes! Yes!" Dr. Watson captures the pathway to a vibrant and vital future Wesleyan Methodist movement that desires nothing but humble holiness and changed lives. I'm convinced this book—and more importantly the move of the Holy Spirit for which it yearns—can and will empower a new generation of Methodists that are wholly sanctified to God's glory!

—**Rev. Steven Taylor**, Lead Pastor
Panama United Methodist Church, Panama, New York

Perfect Love expands Watson's seminal work on the class and band meetings by orienting Methodism's peculiar practices to their goal: the radical indwelling of divine love in the heart of the faithful. With historical and theological sensitivity, Watson makes a compelling case for a doctrinally vivified Methodism, and invites us to embark on it here and now.

—**Justus H. Hunter**, PhD, Assistant Professor of Church History
United Theological Seminary, Dayton, Ohio

There is more to the Christian life than so many of us have experienced or ever expected, as Kevin Watson shows us here. This resource provides a clear and compelling call for the spiritual heirs of John Wesley to remember who we are—and whose we are—and to share the message of God's perfect love with the world. Come, Holy Spirit!

—**Ken Loyer**, PhD, Senior Pastor, Spry Church, York, Pennsylvania

Perfect Love hits the sanctification bull's-eye! Kevin Watson does a dynamic job of dissecting the misunderstood and underappreciated secret to a life filled with the power and love of the Holy Spirit. He takes us into doctrine and discipline to understand entire sanctification, and then calls us to preach it and experience it as John Wesley expected early Methodists to do. This is the DNA strand that Methodism needs to recover!

—**Rev. Tim Johnson**, Senior Pastor
Pfrimmer's Chapel United Methodist Church, Corydon, Indiana

Dr. Kevin Watson's *Perfect Love* gives an excellent contemporary practical overview of entire sanctification, the grand depositum, a core doctrine of the Wesleyan/Methodist stream. At this critical time in the United Methodist Church in particular, the various future parts of the church need to consider carefully how this core doctrine will be fleshed out in their new families.

—**Rev. Frank Billman**, DMin, Mentor for the Doctor of Ministry
in Supernatural Ministry, United Theological Seminary, Dayton Ohio

In *Perfect Love*, Kevin Watson offers an even plainer account of Christian perfection. Reengaging the doctrine of entire sanctification under the power of the Spirit will be key for the new Methodism.

—**Rev. Bob Kaylor**, DMin, Lead Pastor
Tri-Lakes United Methodist Church, Monument, Colorado

Entire sanctification is not only a hidden jewel of Wesleyanism, but also a cornerstone of our organization as Methodists and a key to our abandoned passion. Dr. Watson presents a cogent introduction to the Wesleyan concept of Christian perfection with contemporary interpretation and original sources. Those across the Methodist family desiring to reclaim our heritage in the pursuit of holiness will find *Perfect Love* a useful resource and discussion guide.

—**Bishop Jeffrey N. Leath**, 128th Bishop,
The African Methodist Episcopal Church (AME), Nashville, Tennessee

It is not too controversial of a claim to say that John Wesley was difficult to understand on the question of entire sanctification or Christian perfection. And yet, the doctrine is central to Methodist identity. This combination of both ambiguity and centrality has left Wesley's progeny with a choice: either ignore the doctrine or seek vigilantly to invigorate it time and time again. Watson's latest book does the latter, and we should be grateful for it. The people called Methodist must live into the fullness of their theological heritage in order that their identity mean something that can last. *Perfect Love* is a wonderful aide in this regard. I hope it will be a book that is widely read by serious and earnest members of the Wesleyan Methodist tradition.

—**Daniel Castelo**, PhD, Professor of Theology and Methodist Studies
Duke Divinity School, Durham, North Carolina

In *Perfect Love*, Kevin Watson calls the larger Wesleyan family to imagine the impact of a renewal of the Wesleyan doctrine of entire sanctification. He reminds us of the promise of the full gospel, namely deliverance from sin and transformation of the affections. I join with the author in praying for a revival of holy love, and the flourishing of pure religion.

—**Cheryl Bridges Johns**, PhD,
Professor of Spiritual Renewal and Christian Formation
Pentecostal Theological Seminary, Cleveland, Tennessee

Here is an excellent recovery of the vital doctrine in Wesleyanism. Kevin Watson has done us a great service in this important book. Scripture, history, doctrine, and the work of the sanctifying Holy Spirit as the way to renewal for all of us in the Methodist family. Read this book! It will enrich how you think and pray and minister as we move ahead in the spirit of John Wesley.

—**Steven Hoskins**, PhD., Professor of Christian History,
Trevecca Nazarene University, Nashville, Tennessee

Kevin Watson believes and knows that God can bring change in the inner heart and outward actions of a person. In a warm, personal, and conversational manner, Dr. Watson examines and explains John Wesley's call to entire sanctification and encourages readers to discover the blessed life that God has in store for them. It is well worth the journey to read and to listen to this book.

—**Rev. Martin Nicholas**, Senior Pastor
Sugar Land United Methodist Church, Sugar Land, Texas

The main value of Kevin Watson's *Perfect Love* is not that he articulates so well the meaning of Wesley's teaching about entire sanctification, but that he inspires us and shows us how to appropriate this teaching for ourselves and for the church today. Methodism began and grew with a distinctive message about becoming holy by God's grace through faith, and it is this message that is necessary for Methodists and all Christians today. In the end a recovery of Wesley's thought matters little if there is no appropriation of the Wesleyan way of salvation and of Christian living.

—**Timothy W. Whitaker**, Bishop, retired,
Southeastern Jurisdiction, The United Methodist Church

Through the worldwide Methodist family and its commitment to a Wesleyan understanding of sanctification, people from Nigeria to New Zealand and from Cuba to Congo, have experienced deep and abiding Holy Spirit–inspired change in their lives. I am deeply grateful to Kevin Watson for providing a clear and hopeful vision of the fullness of salvation, and pray that the North American part of our global family would be emboldened by his words to reclaim the power of the Holy Spirit DNA that lies at the heart of our movement.

—**Kimberly D. Reisman**, Executive Director,
World Methodist Evangelism, West Lafayatte, Indiana

Perfect Love urges the people known as Methodists to reclaim the power of their faith—entire sanctification or holiness. He grounds his premise in Scripture and uses the words of John Wesley to remind us of the divine calling God has placed on us to model Christian perfection. The gift of this book is that Watson ends with a strong note of hopefulness that we will return to this faith quest and provides some very simple ways for individuals and groups to begin the journey.

—**Bishop Teresa Jefferson-Snorton**, Presiding Bishop, Fifth Episcopal District,
The Christian Methodist Episcopal Church (CME), Birmingham, Alabama

In this epic work, Kevin Watson expresses a clarion call for Methodist Christians to reclaim our understanding and experience of entire sanctification. Too many descendents of Wesley live in a spiritual anemia rooted in a lack of comprehension of the grand depositum of the Methodist movement. Because of the deep brokenness we find within the human condition in our time, much is at stake in understanding the truths contained in this work. Whether you are a pastor or layperson, God stands ready to empower you in overcoming the debilitating forces of sin and entering into the joyful liberation of being perfected in love in this life. This book should not be ignored by anyone who desires to see the church restored as a city on a hill through seeking God in justification *and* sanctification and helping others do the same

—**Rev. Paul Lawler**, Lead Pastor, Christ Church UMC, Birmingham, Alabama

In *Perfect Love*, Watson ably argues that Methodism's identity crisis is rooted in our neglect of teaching and preaching entire sanctification. He combines his own small-group experience with John Wesley's teaching to suggest that the future vitality of Methodism depends on recovering this most distinctive doctrine. His argument is persuasive and important for all Christians today.

—**Bishop Scott Jones**, Resident Bishop of the Texas Conference
Houston Episcopal Area, The United Methodist Church

I sense that the Methodist movement is going through a season of doctrinal and theological renewal where truths that have been lost, forgotten or abandoned are reclaimed as God brings revival to His church. Kevin Watson has ensured that we will not suffer from theological amnesia with respect to one of God's wonderful promises and our great hope to be realized in this life–God's desire that we be sanctified completely. The church owes Kevin Watson our deep gratitude for fanning the flames of renewal and revival with this book which clearly presents the doctrine of Christian perfection for our generation. May God use it to produce Perfect Love in our lives and witness for such a time as this.

—**Rev. Keith Boyette**, President, Wesleyan Covenant Association and
Chair, Transitional Leadership Council of the Global Methodist Church

Grounded in the historical and theological narratives of the Methodist tradition, the author calls for reclaiming the Wesleyan vision of perfect love that rightly compels today's church to embody the scriptural holiness encapsulated in the teaching and promotion of entire sanctification. Beyond the circles of the Methodists, the call to recover entire sanctification propels a shared, ecumenical vision of the Christian life that celebrates the fresh outpouring of the Holy Spirit and the newness of life it generates. Written in a plain language, the author provides an invigorating portrayal of Wesley's message on entire sanctification and the optimism of grace inherently operative in such conception of the Christian life. For ministry practitioners in today's church, this book is a must read.

—**David Sang-Ehil Han**, PhD, Dean of the Faculty and Vice-President for Academics,
Pentecostal Theological Seminary, Cleveland, Tennessee

PERFECT LOVE

Recovering Entire Sanctification—The Lost Power of the Methodist Movement

KEVIN M. WATSON

Printed in the United States of America

Cover design by Strange Last Name
Page design and layout by PerfecType, Nashville, Tennessee

Watson, Kevin M.
Perfect love : recovering entire sanctification : the lost power of the Methodist movement / Kevin M. Watson. – Franklin, Tennessee : Seedbed Publishing, ©2021.

pages ; cm. + 1 videodisc

ISBN 9781628248081 (paperback)
ISBN 9781628244854 (DVD)
ISBN 9781628248098 (Mobi)
ISBN 9781628248104 (ePub)
ISBN 9781628248111 (uPDF)
OCLC 1246361946

1. Sanctification. 2. Methodist Church -- Doctrines. I. Title. II. Series.

BT765.W38 2021 234.8 2021937326

SEEDBED PUBLISHING
Franklin, Tennessee
seedbed.com

To Lesly Broadbent, Matthew Johnson, Matt Judkins,
and Andrew Thompson

Six months before his death, John Wesley wrote a letter to an influential Methodist preacher concerning the supreme importance of the doctrine of entire sanctification on the power of the Methodist movement:

> I am glad brother D— has more light with regard to full sanctification. This doctrine is the grand depositum which God has lodged with the people called Methodists; and for the sake of propagating this chiefly He appeared to have raised us up.
>
> —John Wesley
>
> *Letter to Robert Carr Brackenbury, September 15, 1790*[1]

The following extract was found in handwritten manuscript notes by Oswald Chambers for a book titled *The Gospel Mystery of Sanctification*. Chambers died without the book being published. Oswald Chambers, the author of numerous books, is best known for his classic devotional *My Utmost for His Highest.*

> There was one doctrine of John Wesley's—the doctrine of perfect sanctification—which ought to have led to a great and original ethical development; but the doctrine has not grown; it seems to remain just where John Wesley left it. There has been want of the genius or courage to attempt the solution of the immense practical questions which the doctrine suggests. The questions have not been raised—much less solved. To have raised them effectively, indeed, would have been to originate an ethical revolution which would have had a far deeper effect on the thought and life—first of England, and then of the rest of Christendom—than was produced by the Reformation of the sixteenth century.
>
> —R. W. Dale
>
> *The Evangelical Revival*[2]

Contents

Foreword

The phrase "entire sanctification" was very common in my upbringing. Throughout my childhood growing up in an American Holiness–influenced denomination, sanctification was part of regular preaching. It generally meant "two trips to the altar"—one to get saved and one to get sanctified.

Shortly after I graduated from college and married my husband, Wayne, we set out to lead our first church. We both felt a strong calling and were eager to reach people for Jesus. We worked hard. I taught school to assist in the income, but my heart was in growing the church. It was not long before reality set in. I was no longer the preacher's kid; I was the preacher.

I had a constant gnawing in my spirit that there had to be something more. Even though it was difficult to explain, I finally decided that the best way to get rid of this inner pain was to persuade Wayne to leave the ministry. Over dinner one night I said how wonderful it would be to have the capacity to give away a lot of money and help many people. Then I suggested that his leaving the ministry and selling insurance might be a good way to do this. I was not prepared for the immediate response. Looking me straight in the eyes he slowly articulated, "Jo Anne, I don't know what you are going to do, but God has called me to preach and that is what I have to do." End of conversation.

My restless spirit did not end. One day returning from school and washing my hands, I heard God say, "Jo Anne, you need to get your spiritual life in order."

I responded audibly, "I can't right now. I have to get this Christmas program ready at church. Maybe in February I can think about it." I really did not think this was anything spiritual. After all, I knew everything there was to know about all this stuff.

Many Sundays I would wake up ill. I strongly disliked attending church and more and more disliked the people. A rather difficult place to be when one is a pastor! It didn't occur to me to connect the dots of a spiritual need because I had always followed all the rules. Yes, I knew about John Wesley's heart-warming experience. I had heard it preached many times. But that did not apply to me in the way I had arranged my spirituality.

One morning I woke up quite ill and it was not Sunday. Wayne scooped me up and took me to the emergency room. They put me in the ICU and said I would need immediate surgery on my stomach. Wayne had been wanting me to read Catherine Marshall's book *Beyond Ourselves*, but I resisted. In my mind I thought, *What can she teach me? She is Presbyterian and I know everything there is to know*. But somehow in my desperation that day I asked him to bring me the book. My arrogance still in charge, I wanted to look at the chapters first to see if it was even worthwhile. My eyes fell on the chapter, "Ego Slaying" and as I read, God began to speak to my heart. I began to confess my sins of pride, arrogance, self-promotion, greed, selfishness, self-sufficiency, and on and on. In fact, it felt to me as if God put a big screen in front of me and wrote them down. I was broken. I became so hungry for God that all I wanted was Him. I had never been this hungry for God. I had no label from my limited theology and didn't care.

Miraculously, I did not need surgery and after a few days was sent home. The hunger and openness to God continued though. I started reading Scripture. Not to check it off my discipline list, but to know God. I began to read the Holiness classics. Frankly, I did not expect anything; I just simply knew I was hungry and seeking God and He would receive me.

A month later I was leading the Wednesday night prayer meeting. In all honesty I did not like attending these meetings. They were frustrating to me. Everyone gave the same testimony and in addition I did not like the people. We began singing the old hymn "Satisfied" by Clara Teare Williams. Suddenly it was as if wave after wave of the Spirit of God came over me. I wept and began confessing to the people how I had not liked them and had not liked to come to church. I could not believe the words tumbling out of my mouth. The people were stunned. They had never had a pastor talk like this! But the greater thing is that God gave me love for the people that night that I could have never conjured up myself. I began to tell them how much I loved them. I saw them in a totally different light. His love filled that little church that night and continued over the years in more ways than I have space to write.

That night in that little church in Springfield, Missouri, in January of 1965 was the beginning of my journey of the sanctified life. A new lens in seeing others and the world through the eyes of Jesus that continues to this day.

As I read *Perfect Love* my heart leapt within me. My imagination cannot grasp the enormous outpouring God would do in this generation and those to come if we recover entire sanctification. May it be so Lord!

Jo Anne Lyon,
General Superintendent Emeritas
The Wesleyan Church

Acknowledgments

This book is my attempt to bring ideas that are not my own back to the forefront of the broad Methodist family. I am indebted to all who have gone before me and have preached, taught, and written about Methodism's "grand depositum," or great gift, of entire sanctification. I am genuinely grateful to be, in some small way, a steward of Methodism's theological heritage. It is beautiful and worth giving our best thought and attention.

The idea for this book came from a conversation with Andy Miller at Seedbed. Since my first book with Seedbed, it has been a blessing to be able to call Andy a friend and partner in ministry. Andy not only planted the seed for the need for a book like this, he also put far more time and energy than usual into reading multiple drafts and providing helpful comments about the structure of the book and often more detailed editorial comments. He has also been exceptionally patient with me throughout this process. Thank you, Andy, for your friendship and support of this project. Thanks are also due to the team at Seedbed for their hard work and determination to "sow for a great awakening." May it be so!

I want to publicly thank the key mentors who first taught me about entire sanctification, which is not intended to suggest that they will necessarily agree with everything that follows. Doug Strong was the first seminary professor who taught this doctrine in a way that grabbed my attention from that day to the present. Scott Kisker was the other key professor of mine when I was in seminary who strengthened and confirmed my understanding of Methodist doctrine. I also want to thank William J. Abraham for ways that he challenged and sharpened my understanding of entire sanctification. Daniel Castelo was a crucial conversation partner when we were colleagues together at Seattle Pacific University. Thank you, Doug, Scott, Billy, and Daniel.

A number of people have read parts or the entirety of this manuscript or have been important conversation partners along the way. I am especially thankful to Justus Hunter, Stephen Rankin, and Ken Loyer for the time and energy they have given to discussing all things Methodist.

As always, I could not do any of this without the love, support, and care of my family. Thank you, in particular, is due to my wife, Melissa, and to my kids, Bethany, James, and Eden. Though you all know better than anyone how much room I still have to grow, it is my prayer that these words come alive in each of our lives.

Finally, I want to thank the men in my current band meeting: Lesly Broadbent, Matthew Johnson, Matt Judkins, and Andrew Thompson. You all have been a tangible and invaluable source of support and encouragement over the past several years. You have encouraged me to earnestly strive after entire sanctification. God has heard and often answered your prayers on my behalf. I give thanks to God for bringing us together. Words fail me when I try to express how much you all mean to me. This book is dedicated to you four with love and gratitude.

Prologue

I remember the first time I heard someone give a detailed explanation of Methodism's "grand depositum," the doctrine of entire sanctification. I was a seminary student preparing to become a pastor. And after Dr. Doug Strong's lecture was finished, I knew I now had the vocabulary to give voice to things I knew I believed but couldn't express.

The Methodist theological tradition gave me the framework I needed to express the hope, optimism, and possibility for deep transformation in Christ that I read about in Scripture.

This book is about a core belief that John Wesley was convinced was the reason the Holy Spirit breathed life in the people called Methodists. We were created to bring this belief to the church and plant it as deeply as we could in the souls of as many people's lives as possible.

This belief is radical because it professes that radical change *in this life* is possible *by the grace of God*.

Ever since that class more than a decade and a half ago, I have been hoping and praying to see a revival of entire sanctification in the church. I want people to hear about this teaching. I want it to be taught across the church. But more than that, I want to see a revival of the experience of freedom from the power of sin in the lives of Christ-followers that comes by the amazing grace of God.

I want to see a generation of Christians experience all that God has for them.

In the pages that come, I am going to do everything I can to convince you that there is more to the Christian life than you may have experienced or even expected.

I want to give you fair warning that there will be times I say things that may sound crazy or unbelievable to you. When this happens, I am doing the best that I can to be faithful to the teaching of Scripture and the Wesleyan theological heritage. I hope you will explore both for yourself and hold me accountable to them.

I am passionate about this book because I believe the Christian faith is much more than forgiveness of sins and pardon—though it is certainly that. And I do not by any means intend to suggest that justification is trivial.

I believe those who are in Christ are offered full salvation—a salvation that addresses past sin and offers freedom from the power of sin in the present.

And this is really Methodism's big idea: salvation brings not only forgiveness and pardon but also empowerment and freedom to live a faithful and holy life *entirely* and *right now*. This is our grand depositum—the treasure that God has entrusted to the particular people called Methodists.

I have wanted to write a book like this for a long time. I don't think I've ever been more excited to write something. I have also struggled with this book more than any other because this book gets at my deep hope and passion for Methodism's theological heritage. Entire sanctification is the beautiful treasure that God has entrusted to us.

I have done the very best I could to do justice to our grand depositum. But as I've written I've been deeply aware of my own shortcomings as a pastor, teacher, and author.

Because this book is about the doctrine and experience of entire sanctification, I also need to be upfront with you that I am writing about a doctrine I believe in but have not yet experienced. Writing this book has increased my awareness of my desperate need for God and my hunger for God to do in me what I cannot do in myself.

I hope and pray it does the same for you. May God graciously give us faith and expectation to be filled to overflowing with love for God and other people. I'd like to end with a powerful quote in which John Wesley expresses emphatically the unparalleled significance of love in Methodist theology:

> [One cause of] a thousand mistakes is [this:] . . . not considering deeply enough that love is the highest gift of God; humble, gentle, patient love; that all visions, revelations, [or] manifestations whatever, are little things compared to love; and that all [other] gifts . . . are either the same with or infinitely inferior to it.
>
> [Y]ou should be thoroughly [aware] of this—the heaven of heavens is love. There is nothing higher in religion; there is, in effect, nothing else; if you look for anything but more love, you are looking wide of the mark, you are getting out of the royal way. And when you are

asking others, "Have you received this or that blessing?" if you mean anything but more love, you mean wrong; you are leading them out of the way, and putting them [on] a false scent. Settle it then in your heart, that from the moment God has saved you from all sin, you are to aim at nothing more but more of that love described in the thirteenth [chapter] of [First] Corinthians. You can go no higher than this, till you are carried into Abraham's bosom.

—John Wesley

from "A Plain Account of Christian Perfection"[1]

PERFECT LOVE

1

A Crisis of Identity—We Have Forgotten Who We Are

Methodism is in the midst of an identity crisis. We have forgotten who we are. We have abandoned our theological heritage. In the pages that follow, I will make a simple argument: above all else, God raised up the people called Methodists to preach, teach, and experience one core doctrine. This doctrine is Methodism's reason for existence. If we get this right, everything else will fall into place. If we get it wrong, we will miss the unique calling and purpose that God has for us.

Less than six months before he died, John Wesley wrote a letter to Robert Carr Brackenbury that referred to this core doctrine as "the grand depositum which God has lodged with the people called Methodists; and for the sake of propagating this chiefly He appeared to have raised us up."[1]

That sounds important! But the previous quotation also contains a handful of words that we do not use much today. Let's start with "grand depositum." Wesley meant that God had deposited or entrusted Methodism with something of great worth and importance. Propagating means to spread or pass on to others. So, Wesley was saying that God had entrusted Methodism with something specific of great worth and importance. And God raised up Methodism in order to spread what God has entrusted to us to as many other people as possible.

Wesley identified the key thing that God gave to Methodists as a specific doctrine or teaching. So, what is this doctrine? Entire sanctification or Christian perfection is the grand depositum that God has given to us. This book is an attempt to bring entire sanctification back to the forefront of Methodism.

Entire sanctification is the doctrine that defines Methodism's audacious optimism that the grace of God saves us entirely, to the uttermost.

I hope to convince you that this grand depositum is *still* the reason God raised up Methodists. Methodism exists in order to preach, teach, and proclaim the bold optimism that the grace of God is able to bring full salvation to everyone. Methodism separated from this core teaching has no future. If Methodism focuses once again on this grand depositum, it will find new life and fresh outpouring of the Holy Spirit in its midst.

We have the opportunity to recover this powerful truth and again present it to a world desperate for hope and healing. How exciting!

Before we go any farther, let me say a word about what I mean by "Methodist" or "Methodism" in this book. This book is for everyone who at some point traces their spiritual lineage back to John Wesley, the founder of Methodism. It is probably most obvious that this includes denominations that have the word *Methodist* in their names, such as the United Methodist Church[2] or the African Methodist Episcopal Church. I also have members of the Holiness Movement in mind, like the Wesleyan Church, the Free Methodist Church, Church of God (Anderson), Church of the Nazarene, and the Salvation Army. But this is still not the full extent of the Methodist family. I am also thinking of members of the global Pentecostal movement whose understanding of a second work of grace and baptism of the Holy Spirit can be traced back to John Wesley and the doctrine of entire sanctification. When Pentecostalism is taken into consideration, we are talking about well more than a billion (yes, billion with a "b") Christians today who can trace their heritage back to Wesley and early Methodism.

Methodism's significance within the body of Christ is often underestimated or overlooked. But we are a powerful movement of the Holy Spirit that has brought not only forgiveness of sins through faith in Christ, but also freedom from the power of sin and an outpouring of holy love in countless lives over the past three centuries. Methodism has been the most Spirit-filled in our history when people have leaned into our grand depositum and wrestled with God to help people receive the blessing of entire sanctification. When Methodists have lowered their expectations of what God can do in this life, spiritual and numeric decline have followed.

God did not raise us up to lower expectation for what is possible through the work of Jesus Christ. We have been brought to life to tell the world that "it is God's will that you should be sanctified" (1 Thess. 4:3a). And God is able to do what he wants to do in us!

Why Are We Here?

These are trying times for Wesley's spiritual heirs. All who trace their spiritual lineage back to John Wesley are facing sustained challenges in a variety of ways. Despite these real and serious challenges, I feel excitement and a growing sense of anticipation. I have an expectation in my spirit that the living God is going to do an (old) new thing.

Unsettled and even chaotic times can provide an opportunity for reevaluation. They can bring clarity. Difficult seasons can bring renewed focus on the reason a group exists. This is a great time to seek clarity about a basic question: Why are we here?

I am convinced that there is one main reason we exist: to preach, teach, and help people receive the gift of entire sanctification. This is the reason God first breathed life into Methodism. And this is the reason I have hope God will breathe life into our churches once again.

Return[3]

Like many of you, I've been praying. I've been asking God to break through. I've been wrestling with what faithfulness looks like in this time and in this place. And I've been hearing the word *return*. The first time I heard that word, my mind was going in so many different directions I wasn't sure what it meant. But as I've kept hearing *return*, the mist and confusion have been clearing away and one particular Scripture passage has stood out:

> Thus says the LORD:
> Stand at the crossroads, and look,
> and ask for the ancient paths,

> where the good way lies; and walk in it,
> and find rest for your souls.
> But they said, "We will not walk in it." (Jer. 6:16 NRSV)

It is time for the people called Methodists and all of John Wesley's spiritual heirs to return to the ancient path that Wesley referred to as the "grand depositum" of "the people called Methodists." Lest we respond like those who heard Jeremiah: "But they said, 'We will not walk in it.'"

The grand depositum of Methodism was the doctrine of entire sanctification, or Christian perfection. The mission of Methodism in Britain and in the United States was initially to "spread scriptural holiness." Holiness, or sanctification, was the core focus and purpose of the people called Methodists. Wesley understood holiness to be an ongoing process of becoming more and more like Jesus, loving God and neighbor to the exclusion of sin. Entire sanctification (which will also be referred to as Christian perfection or full salvation here) was the goal of ongoing growth in holiness. So, what exactly is entire sanctification? In *A Plain Account of Christian Perfection*, Wesley gave a succinct definition:

> (1) That Christian perfection is that love of God and our neighbor, which implies deliverance from all sin. (2) That this is received merely by faith. (3) That it is given instantaneously, in one moment. (4) That we are to expect it, not at death, but every moment; that now is the accepted time, now is the day of this salvation.[4]

The goal for Wesley and his followers was to actually live the kind of life that Scripture tells us is possible by the grace of God in Christ Jesus. This determination was expressed most boldly in the doctrine of entire sanctification. This teaching was the grand depositum that God gave to Wesley and those who went before us.

It is time to return, to recommit to steward what has been entrusted to those who follow in the footsteps of Wesley and the first Methodists.

The Stakes Are High

I am convinced that any form of Methodism that is not clearly connected to the doctrine of entire sanctification has no future. Any new movements or expressions of Methodism must place our grand depositum at the center of our faith and practice. I am equally convinced that if we as a people recommit ourselves to this grand depositum, God will breathe new life into our movement out of love for a desperate and hurting world.

Here is what I see as being at stake for us today: We live in a world where many are desperate for hope and healing. Many have a quiet desperation that comes from the numbness and pseudo connections that have developed from spending too much time connected to our screens and far too little time connecting in person in life-giving relationships. Many are desperate because they know that their lives are going in directions that are not going to end well, but they are not able to stop. Many are depressed, discouraged, and simply without hope. The list could go on.

In this reality, our calling is to preach the full gospel. We have the good news of Jesus Christ. The gospel of Jesus not only brings forgiveness and pardon; the gospel brings hope and healing. Through faith in the amazing grace of God, we can be forgiven and reconciled to God. This is, indeed, good news. But there is more! God doesn't want to just forgive us, he also wants to offer us power and freedom over the ways of sin and death. We need not limp through this life, defeated, merely surviving. No! "We are more than conquerors through him who loved us" (Rom. 8:37 NRSV)!

We can be saved to the uttermost!

Jesus Is Able

There should not be a church in any of our communities that has a more audacious and bold optimism of what God's grace can do in the lives of every single person than churches that trace their roots back to John Wesley. Entire sanctification is not an abstract idea or merely a theory.

Not at all!

Entire sanctification is the fruit that comes from knowing a person—Jesus, our risen Lord. Jesus saves. Jesus rescues. Jesus heals. He has done these things before and he will do them again!

There is still Living Water here.

As we unplug the well of entire sanctification and invite people to drink deeply from it, we will see fruit. We will see lives undone by the love of God that has been poured out over the world in Jesus Christ. We will see lives mended and made whole. We can unplug this well now and offer the Water that is already in it today to the people in our communities.

For those confused by my connection of Methodism to Pentecostalism, it may be helpful to realize that John Fletcher (1729–1785) was a key spokesperson for John Wesley during Wesley's lifetime. (Fletcher actually died before Wesley, though he was younger than him.) When Fletcher wrote about the possibilities of entire sanctification or Christian perfection, he often referred to it as baptism in the Holy Spirit (or Holy Ghost). This language echoed through the generations until the second blessing of entire sanctification was picked up in the beginnings of Pentecostalism and found new life and new development.

Once Pentecostalism became a major movement, baptism in the Holy Spirit quickly became associated, if not synonymous, with the Pentecostal emphasis on speaking in tongues. One way this is seen in Methodist history was when the Church of the Nazarene changed the first part of their original name, Pentecostal Church of the Nazarene, once it became clear that "Pentecostal" was firmly connected to glossolalia in most people's minds. Nazarenes did not embrace the Pentecostal emphasis on speaking in tongues as a sign of a second blessing of being filled with the Spirit. Despite this different emphasis, the two traditions nevertheless have the same theological roots.

One of the foremost historians of the Holiness-Pentecostal tradition, Vinson Synan, has argued that, "Pentecostalism was basically a modified 'second blessing' Methodist spirituality that was pioneered by John Wesley and passed down to his followers in the holiness movement, out of which came the modern Pentecostal movement."[5]

Before those of us who are not connected to Pentecostal churches are too quick to reject Pentecostalism as a part of our extended family, we would do well to remember that ecstatic experiences were common in early Methodism. Methodists would often experience things that looked nearly identical to what would today be described as falling out or being slain in the Spirit. The Holy Spirit often showed up in surprising and unpredictable ways when Methodists gathered for worship! We will see multiple examples of this in the following pages.

One of the best-known examples occurred less than a year after John Wesley's famous experience that happened on May 24, 1738, at Aldersgate Street.

Wesley and a variety of key leaders (including George Whitefield and Charles Wesley) in the beginning of the Methodist revival in England were meeting together at the Fetter Lane Society for a love feast on New Year's Eve. A love feast was a time of sharing a light meal and testifying to how they had seen God at work in their lives. There were about sixty people who had gathered together to pray and testify to the goodness of God. And then the Holy Spirit came upon them in a powerful and unexpected way. Here is John Wesley's account of what happened:

> About three in the morning, as we were continuing instant in prayer, the power of God came mightily upon us, insomuch that many cried out for exceeding joy, and *many fell to the ground*. As soon as we were recovered a little from that awe and amazement at the presence of his majesty, we broke out with one voice, "We praise thee, O God; we acknowledge thee to be the Lord."[6]

This account sounds like what Pentecostals and charismatics would describe as "falling out" under the power of the Holy Spirit.

And many Wesleyans and Methodists who are desperate for God to do a new work in their lives are encountering God in powerful, supernatural, and life-changing ways today. I have seen this myself at Seedbed's New Room Conference, which started meeting annually in September 2014. God has been present in powerful and life-changing ways at New Room, with powerful manifestations of the Holy Spirit. A host of testimonies have come out of New Room of people who have experienced inner healing, physical healing, and freedom from addiction, as well as people being filled with the Holy Spirit. It has been a place of renewal, restoration, and healing.[7]

It is not surprising that this conference started with a core commitment to lift up the full gospel.

The yearly Aldersgate Conference is another place where people hungry for more of God are being filled with God's presence. It was at an Aldersgate Conference in Tulsa, Oklahoma, that a close friend of mine went to the event, by his own account, a bit of a skeptic. But the Lord met him there and delivered him from a long-term addiction to chewing tobacco. As of this writing, he has not used tobacco in well over a year.[8]

It is always risky to mention specific examples like these in a book like this. They tend to become dated quickly and then date the book itself. I share these here, despite that risk, to illustrate that people are hungry for encounters with the living God today, just as they were in eighteenth-century Methodism. And though these may soon be outdated, new expressions will doubtless arise to replace them.

A Road Map for the Rest of This Book

Okay, I hope I have your attention! My goal is straightforward: I want to convince you to boldly press into our grand depositum.

The central importance of Christian perfection in the history of Methodism is not just a theoretical idea, it is a doctrine that many Methodists experienced and testified to with joy and exultation.

The rest of this book is divided into two main parts. The first part gives you a sense of the central place of the doctrine of entire sanctification for John Wesley and the first Methodists. You will encounter several testimonies of Christians who experienced full salvation. These demonstrate that this was a living word for those who have gone before us. I hope they will also awaken a desire in you to press in with God in prayer to seek all that God has for you. The decline of entire sanctification in Methodist theology and experience will also be briefly discussed in order to help us understand where we are.

The second part is intended to deepen our understanding of what exactly it is that we are after. What is and is not meant by entire sanctification? And how can we receive this precious gift today?

If you are satisfied with your life and content with where you are, then this book may not be for you. But if you have a sense that God has more for you, then *this book is for you*. If you know that part of your life is not the way that God intends for it to be and if you are hungry and thirsty for more of God, *this book is for you*. If you are desperate and ready to experience, as my friend J. D. Walt often says, the rest of the gospel—then *this book is most definitely for you*.

Now is always the time to boldly pursue all that God has for us. Methodists have left our theological heritage in a musty basement or in a forgotten chest in the attic for far too long. It is time to retrieve and receive the grand depositum that God has so graciously given to us.

As I've written these pages, I've worried that I may seem negative or pessimistic about the future. Please know that I have written this book with a deep hope and optimism for what is possible by the grace of God.

I am a Methodist because I believe, by the grace of God and the power of the resurrection of Jesus Christ, that we can experience complete freedom from sin and death now. I am a Methodist because I believe we have been entrusted with the most audacious, bold, and positive vision for the possibilities of transformation that are available on this side of Easter.

I am a Methodist because I do not believe that the Christian life must be one of futility or frustration, where one does the best one can but is not able to completely give one's life in obedience to Christ. By faith in Jesus, all who are created in the image of God can experience not only the joy of having our sin canceled, but the deeper joy of experiencing God break the power of canceled sin, as Charles Wesley so eloquently put it.

Teaching and preaching the possibility of being made perfect in love for God and neighbor, and seeking to actually become entirely sanctified are the reasons Methodism was raised up.

May we remember who we are and why the Holy Spirit brought us to life!

Come, Holy Spirit, breathe life into your people once more.

Small Group Discussion Guide

My hope is that this book will serve not only as an individual resource for greater understanding of the doctrine of entire sanctification and its central role in Methodist theology, but that it will also be used in small groups to study Methodism's grand depositum. More important, I hope people will come together to support, encourage, and pray for one another, pressing into the heart of God for complete salvation.

In hopes of facilitating group discussion, a guide is included at the end of each chapter. There will be a handful of discussion questions to help kickstart your conversation and to further explore the concepts in the book.

Throughout the history of Methodism, many denominations have asked a series of questions of those who are pursuing ordained ministry. Three of the first four questions relate specifically to the doctrine of entire sanctification, or Christian perfection. They are:

> Are you going on to perfection?
> Do you expect to be made perfect in love in this life?
> Are you earnestly striving after perfection in love?[9]

Since this book is intended to not merely be about an idea, but to encourage the pursuit of entire sanctification, the final question each week focuses on your own pursuit of entire sanctification. This guide, then, will give each group member a chance to weigh in on the extent to which they have been earnestly striving after perfection in love.

The point of this last question is not to try to outdo one another. It is to provide a place to tell the truth in hopes of lovingly encouraging each other to take the next step in pursuing all that God has for us. I know in my own life there have been times when my honest answer to that question would have been: "No, I have not been earnestly striving after perfection in love." If that is where you are, it is good to be honest. Progress starts with an honest and realistic assessment of where you are before you can move forward. The goal of this question is mutual support and encouragement to see God break through and to receive the gift of full salvation.

Open with a Prayer

Introductions (15 minutes)

During this time, group members should introduce themselves to each other, as necessary. Begin by sharing what made each person interested in reading this book.

Questions for Discussion (30 minutes)

1. What have your expectations been for your life as a follower of Jesus Christ? How did this chapter impact those expectations?
2. Do you find that the particular part of the broad Methodist tradition that you are in is experiencing a crisis of identity? If not, how would you describe that identity? If so, what are the key convictions that are needed in order for your community to rediscover its identity in Christ?
3. What was most challenging to you about this chapter? Were you more energized or eager to learn and experience more in this chapter?

Are you earnestly striving after perfection in love? (10 minutes)

Each group member should be given an opportunity to answer this question each week. For the first few weeks, it might be helpful to frame the question in this way: On a scale of 1–10, how earnest have you been in striving after perfection in love?

Close with a Prayer

2

Methodism's Purpose

The Purpose of Methodism According to Our Founder

In 1786, about five years before his death, John Wesley wrote a plea to Methodists that summarized what he saw as the essentials for ongoing spiritual vitality. He wrote:

> I am not afraid that the people called Methodists should ever cease to exist either in Europe or America. But I am afraid lest they should only exist as a dead sect, having the form of religion without the power. And *this undoubtedly will be the case unless they hold fast both the doctrine, spirit, and discipline with which they first set out.*[1]

With the benefit of almost half a century of experience leading the Methodist revival, Wesley was adamant that Methodism would continue as a powerful movement of God as long as it "held fast" to the doctrine, spirit, and discipline with which it started. The doctrine of entire sanctification was at the center of Methodist doctrine. This teaching provided the rationale for Methodist discipline.

Two decades before Wesley wrote "Thoughts upon Methodism," he wrote a letter to an early Methodist preacher. After a brief greeting, Wesley got straight to the point:

> Where Christian perfection is not strongly and explicitly preached, there is seldom any remarkable blessing from God; and, consequently, little addition to the society, and little life in the members of it. Therefore, if Jacob Rowell is grown faint, and says but little about it . . . you supply his lack of service. Speak and spare not. Let not regard for any man induce you to betray the truth of God. Till you press the believers to expect *full salvation* NOW, you must not look for any revival.[2]

In a time when we acutely need revival, what would John Wesley say about our present prospects? Based on this letter, he would say we have no right to expect revival because we have not been pressing ourselves—*those who are already connected to Methodism*—to expect full salvation *now*.

Less than a year before his death, John Wesley wrote another letter that once again insisted that entire sanctification was the very reason for Methodism's existence. Wesley started the letter by noting that his health was declining as his "body seems nearly to have done its work and be almost worn out." Perhaps it was facing his impending death that caused Wesley to reflect on the big picture of his life and involvement in Methodism.

It was in this context that Wesley offered the powerful description of why God had "raised up" Methodism, the guiding thesis of this book. Wesley wrote:

> I am glad brother D— has more light with regard to full sanctification. This doctrine is the grand depositum which God has lodged with the people called Methodists; and for the sake of propagating this chiefly He appeared to have raised us up.[3]

As Wesley looked back over the more than fifty years of Methodism and thought about the work that he had seen God do during those years, he zeroed in on this one particular doctrine as the key explanation for why God had done this surprising thing in his lifetime. The belief in entire sanctification, or full sanctification, was *the reason for Methodism*.

Wesley once defined entire sanctification as "purity of intention, dedicating all the life to God. It is the giving God all our heart; it is one desire and design ruling all our tempers."[4] At other times he would equate Christian perfection with the Greatest Commandment in Matthew 22:37–40. When asked by the Pharisees what the greatest commandment in the Law was, Jesus replied: "'Love the Lord your God with all your heart and with all your soul and with all your mind.' This is the first and greatest commandment. And the second is like it: 'Love your neighbor as yourself.' All the Law and the Prophets hang on these two commandments."

Methodism existed because God had given Methodists a particular calling—to preach and teach that through faith in Jesus Christ it is possible to experience full salvation and freedom from sin's power in your life.

Wesley Persisted Even in Adversity

John Wesley was so convinced of the truth of Christian perfection that he continued to make the case for it throughout his life, even though the doctrine was at times a source of controversy. Here is what is so striking to me about this: Wesley is widely viewed by historians as a pragmatist who looked for things that worked in other communities and then used them in Methodism. When things worked, Wesley plugged them in and expanded their role. If something did not work, he was willing to cut his losses and move on.

Wesley relentlessly focused on the growth, development, and expansion of Methodism. He was equally insistent on the quality of Methodist discipleship. Numbers were not good enough; he wasn't trying to raise up a huge crowd of people who were fans of Jesus. Wesley wanted a movement of followers of Jesus, who wholeheartedly pursued holiness, because he was convinced that "without holiness no one will see the Lord" (Heb. 12:14).

Given Wesley's pragmatism, if he insisted that something that caused him problems and enveloped him in controversy throughout his life was nevertheless a nonnegotiable, it seems to me we should pay particular attention.

One Key Doctrine and One Key Discipline

Doctrine (beliefs) and discipline (practice) were the main ways Wesley and early Methodists thought about what God was doing in their midst. The goal was not just right beliefs. Methodists wanted to live rightly, or righteously. Wesley was adamant that right living required a discipline—a rigorous commitment to practicing one's faith through concrete practices—which he referred to as means of grace.[5] Most of the doctrines and disciplines that Wesley would have identified as essential for Methodists were common to all Christians.

From my work as an historian of John Wesley's life and theology, there is one doctrine and one practice Wesley was so convinced were essential that he relentlessly fought for them, even though they sometimes caused controversies and had to be vigorously defended. At times, both of these were sources of frustration and misunderstanding. They were easily misunderstood and often maligned. They required constant attention and vigilance. Nevertheless, Wesley persistently and tenaciously insisted that both were of utmost importance to Methodism.

It was not a coincidence that one was a belief and one was a practice, or a doctrine and a discipline. The doctrine of entire sanctification was connected to the particular discipline of watching over one another in love in small groups called band meetings. Wesley believed that holiness was a communal endeavor. Entire sanctification was best pursued in an intimate fellowship where one put everything on the table, hid nothing, and confessed sin in order to be healed and made holy.

My focus here is on the need to reclaim the doctrine of entire sanctification, in part, because I have already written quite a bit on the band meeting elsewhere.[6] Briefly, the band meeting was a group of three to five men or women who gathered weekly in obedience to James 5:16: "Therefore confess your sins to each other and pray for each other so that you may be healed. The prayer of a righteous person is powerful and effective."

Band meetings were radically honest, intense, and vulnerable. There were a variety of questions that fit in two broad categories that had to be answered before being admitted into a band. The first group of questions focused on whether the new member had faith in Christ and assurance of salvation. The second group of questions focused on whether the new member was willing to have other members of the group speak candidly into their lives on a weekly basis. Once admitted, members answered five questions every week:

1. What known sins have you committed since our last meeting?
2. What temptations have you met with?
3. How were you delivered?
4. What have you thought, said, or done, of which you doubt whether it be sin or not?
5. Have you nothing you desire to keep secret?[7]

As you read these questions, it may be easy to see why there were more Methodists who resisted this practice than there were Methodists who embraced it!

These questions get at what is really going on in our lives. If they are answered honestly, they leave no room for hiding. And yet, despite the resistance by some Methodists and the challenge of maintaining these groups, John Wesley continued to insist that band meetings were essential for the mission and vitality of Methodism. In *A Plain Account of Christian Perfection*, Wesley directly discussed the importance of the band meeting in the context of a broader discussion of the doctrine of Christian perfection:

> If you would avoid schism, observe every rule of the Society, and of the Bands, for conscience' sake. Never omit meeting your Class or Band; never absent yourself from any

> public meeting. These are the very sinews of our Society; and whatever weakens, or tends to weaken, our regard for these, or our exactness in attending them, strikes at the very root of our community.[8]

Wesley again discussed the importance of the band meeting in 1781 in a letter to Edward Jackson. In the letter, Wesley urged Jackson to resurrect band meetings in his society because "no Society [local gathering of Methodists] will continue lively without them."[9]

Wesley was adamant that band meetings were essential because they were the engine of holiness in early Methodism. Only people desperate for freedom from all of the ways that sin has wrapped itself around their lives are willing to own and confess their brokenness to other people. And only people who are that desperate are likely to receive the gift of entire sanctification.

Beliefs and practice were always connected for Wesley.

The band meeting is the single most important thing I have participated in as far as my own growth as a follower of Jesus Christ. I cannot imagine my life without the men who have been in band with me and have walked with me week by week, who have prayed regularly for me and held me accountable.

And yet, as much as I can testify to God using the band meeting to change my life, the truth is that I resisted joining one when I was first invited into a band. I was scared to bring everything into the light. I was afraid if anyone really knew me that they wouldn't be able to really love me.

Does any of this sound familiar?

I am so glad that God gave me the strength (after I ignored the invitation for several weeks) to accept the invitation to join a band meeting. God has used the band meetings I have been in to form lifelong friendships. As one of the guys I am in band with right now recently said, "The band meeting is a greenhouse for growth in holiness. It has been uncomfortable at times, to be sure. But it has been an indescribable blessing in my life!"[10]

If the band meeting was the key practice that facilitated growth in holiness, entire sanctification was the doctrine that sought to describe the full possibility of sanctification. Christians can be, as Wesley's historic questions affirm, "made perfect in love in this life."[11] Entire sanctification points Christians to their intended destination. People who have set their hearts and minds on receiving God's gift of entire sanctification join together with others who have the same commitment to support and encourage each other. This is Methodism at its best and its most powerful.

Methodists Need Each Other

Christians are not formed in isolation. The pursuit of holiness is a communal endeavor. In my mind, one of the biggest problems that contemporary Wesleyan and Methodist faith communities have is rampant individualism that suggests Methodist beliefs (or even basic Christian beliefs) can be embraced or ignored as one so chooses. In too many contexts, there is no foundation of common beliefs and practices that bind a Christian community together. Everything is up for grabs. And if everything is up for grabs, we have a serious identity crisis.

This is especially problematic for Wesley's spiritual heirs. John Wesley defined Methodism through the details of its doctrine and discipline. A Methodist was a person committed to a particular set of beliefs (doctrine) who was committed to living out those beliefs through a particular—and communally agreed upon—way of life (discipline).

This was so important and so foundational to Wesley that he came up with a basic document that provided the basis for a common discipline for every Methodist. This way of life was outlined in a three-page pamphlet. Often referred to as the "General Rules," the document outlined the expectations for everyone who was a member of Methodism.[12]

The rules started by indicating that every Methodist belonged to a small group called a class meeting where they gave money "toward the relief of the poor," discussed the state of their souls (or their present relationship with God), and gave each other advice, encouragement, and held each other accountable to their common way of life.

The General Rules then expressed the lifestyle expectations of Methodists under three main headings. The first General Rule discussed specific sins, or harm, that were to be avoided. This rule included things like "taking the name of God in vain," drunkenness, or laying up treasures on earth. The second General Rule outlined the concrete ways that those connected with John Wesley were expected to do good. Feeding the hungry and visiting the sick are examples of concrete actions that were included under this rule. The third General Rule outlined an expectation that Methodists would consistently practice the means of grace, which included worship, reading Scripture, prayer, fasting, and receiving the Lord's Supper.

The General Rules were a guide to practical holiness. Methodists committed to this specific set of practices because they were pursuing holiness together. They believed Christians grow in their faith when they join together and "watch over one another in love," as Wesley often put it.

A Doctrine That Was Experienced

Throughout John Wesley's life, Methodists not only preached but experienced and testified to the truth and reality of entire sanctification. The testimonies were not dry or boring accounts of a disconnected deity and what that being was theoretically able to do in people's lives.

Far from it!

Methodists experienced God as alive, active, and urgently interested in their lives. At times they were so moved by the love of God that they would cry out and shake. Sometimes they would even fall down and lay prostrate on the floor for hours.

As you can probably imagine, this created something of a scandal in the beginnings of Methodism, particularly with some outspoken critics. Wesley cited one example in his *Journal*:

> We understood that many were offended at the cries of those on whom the power of God came, among whom was a physician, who was much afraid there might be fraud or imposture in the case. Today one whom he had known many years was the first (while I was preaching in Newgate) who broke out into "strong cries and tears." He could hardly believe his own eyes and ears. He went and stood close to her, and observed every symptom, till great drops of sweat ran down her face, and all her bones shook. He then knew not what to think, being clearly convinced it was not fraud, nor yet any natural disorder. But when both her soul and body were healed in a moment, he acknowledged the finger of God.[13]

At other times, they would be so overwhelmed by God's love for them that they would begin to laugh, and the laughter would seem to be uncontrollable for a while. Wesley recorded an instance of he and his younger brother Charles experiencing this in his *Journal*. The brothers were going on a walk and, as they started to sing songs of praise, Charles "burst out into a loud laughter." John started to get angry with his brother, but then began "to laugh as loud as he." Try as they might, neither one of them could stop laughing.[14]

You will be introduced to several testimonies of people who experienced entire sanctification in the pages to come. For now, I want you to see that the doctrine of entire sanctification was sought after with desperation and persistence, oftentimes for weeks, even months. Sometimes this search led people to unexpected encounters with God. The most important thing to know is that when people received the gift of entire sanctification, they all found it was more than worth the wait!

Small Group Discussion Guide

Open with a Prayer

Questions for Discussion

1. How does the summary of Wesley's purpose for Methodism align with your sense of the purpose of Methodism today? What is in alignment with Wesley's purpose? Where do you see a need for realignment?
2. How are the one key doctrine and one key discipline discussed in this chapter connected to each other? Why do you think it was so important to John Wesley that doctrine and discipline be connected and in sync with each other?
3. Do you agree that community is essential for the Christian life? What challenges do individualism and privatization of faith pose for contemporary Methodist communities? What ways can you proactively address those challenges?

Are you earnestly striving after perfection in love?

If it is helpful, use a number from 1–10 to again ease into wrestling with this question. It is okay if it feels uncomfortable to answer this question the first several weeks. Do the best that you can and support and encourage each other!

Close with a Prayer

3

Glimpsing Real Methodism

When I teach on the doctrine of entire sanctification, someone will almost always ask me if I know anyone living who has a testimony to this kind of experience. There is an instinctive feeling that if this doctrine is true, it is the kind of thing that should be evident because people actually experience it and testify to it. My response is usually threefold:

1. I do know some people who have this kind of testimony, though not many at all today.
2. I think that the reason there are so few testimonies to entire sanctification today is because Methodism has put its great treasure under lock and key for far too long. It is difficult for lay Methodists to receive an experience that they have no idea exists.
3. In the periods of Methodist history when this doctrine has been preached with boldness and conviction, it has

never returned empty. Throughout John Wesley's life and ministry and throughout the first decades of Methodism and the Holiness Movement, there are numerous testimonies to entire sanctification in Methodist letters, journals and diaries, and publications of the time.

A Doctrine Experienced

The doctrine of entire sanctification was not merely John Wesley's pet theory or idea. It was a doctrine that was lived out in Methodist experience. No aspect of early Methodist teaching brought more resistance or controversy for John Wesley than did the doctrine of entire sanctification. Wesley continued to urge Methodists to preach, teach, and press after entire sanctification because he was convinced it was biblical and because many Methodists testified to an experience of God's perfect love.

Testimonies to entire sanctification in early Methodism are found in a variety of contexts. Sometimes Methodists felt overwhelmed by their sense of separation from God due to their own sin and unholiness. It was often when their despair at their own ability reached its peak that God broke through and brought glorious victory over their sin and shame. These testimonies are by rank-and-file Methodists who are otherwise unknown to history. And there are also a number of testimonies to entire sanctification by people who became key leaders in Methodism. A number of American Methodist bishops in the nineteenth century, for example, testified to experiencing this doctrine.

Entire sanctification was sometimes experienced when one was alone and wrestling with the Lord in prayer. It also often happened in the context of larger corporate gatherings.

People experienced this breakthrough in Methodist worship services because preachers explicitly preached on this doctrine and exhorted their people to seek after perfection in love. The doctrine also frequently spread when one Methodist testified publicly to an experience of entire sanctification in a communal gathering and then exhorted others to seek what they had themselves found. At times, these testimonies spread like fire on dry stubble. Other accounts of entire sanctification testified to the importance of persisting in continuing to seek the experience, even when someone had not found it after a prolonged period of searching.

"Vile Sinners" Find Clean Hearts

Methodism was organized to "spread Scriptural holiness." This mission was expressed in Methodist preaching and teaching. As we have seen, Methodist belief was characteristically expressed through the structures and organization of the movement. In other words, *Methodism was organized to spread holiness.*

The band meeting may have been the most important context where Methodists gathered together seeking holiness. The meetings were typically sober and serious as members would give a careful and piercing inventory of their lives since they had last met, confessing any conscious sins that they had committed and giving testimony to the ways that God had delivered them from temptation.

Confessing sin week after week would often bring people to a deep sense of their own brokenness before God. They would despair of their ability to rescue themselves. Some Methodists found that it was at this low point that God met them and delivered them from being a "vile sinner," filled them with the perfect love of God that casts out sin, and gave them a clean heart. This was the testimony that Mr. Pritchard shared with his band in 1762, which was reported to Wesley by one of his traveling preachers. In humble faith, Pritchard asked Jesus to give him a clean heart and he heard Jesus say in his spirit, "I will; be thou clean."

As soon as Pritchard heard this word, he also felt a cold and hard bar across his heart break. He then testified: "all my soul was filled with love; nor could I doubt but Jesus had made me clean, through the word which he had spoken to my soul."[1] As often happened in these Methodist meetings, when one person testified to God's work in their lives, many other people had similar experiences. The work of God spread in these communal gatherings like a holy virus.

Experiences like Pritchard's were common in the first generations of British and American Methodism and again throughout the late nineteenth-century Holiness Movement. We have testimonies to entire sanctification from key early Methodist leaders like John Fletcher (1729–1785), Adam Clarke (1762–1832), Jarena Lee (1783–1864), and Phoebe Palmer (1807–1874).

Fletcher was one of the great theologians of Methodism during John Wesley's lifetime. He was influential enough that for a period of time he was actually named as the one who would take over leadership of Methodism on John Wesley's death. (Fletcher ended up dying before Wesley did.) Fletcher testified that through Jesus he was "dead indeed unto sin." He professed that he had taken Jesus "to be my prophet, priest, and king, my indwelling holiness, my all in all."[2]

Adam Clarke was one of the great theologians immediately following the founding generation of British Methodists.

He wrote a number of biblical and theological works that were particularly influential in the first generations of Methodism both in Britain and in the United States. Clarke wrote a letter to Wesley in 1784, describing his desperate determination to have his "heart cleansed from all sin."[3] After experiencing entire sanctification, Clarke found that the experience was difficult to continue to walk in and that he had to seek God's grace continuously to maintain the gift that he had received.

Jarena Lee is one of the most beloved members of the African Methodist Episcopal Church. She is perhaps best known for exercising a preaching ministry at a time when it was almost unheard of for women to preach the gospel. Richard Allen, the founder of the African Methodist Episcopal Church, initially refused to allow Lee to preach. He changed his mind when he heard Lee finish a sermon for a preacher who faltered in the middle of his sermon and was unable to continue. When Allen heard Lee's powerful anointing for himself, he realized he could not stand in the way of the Spirit's work in Lee's life.

Jarena Lee experienced entire sanctification after she had been seeking it for months. One day she began to pray, again, for entire sanctification. As she got up from praying, discouraged that God seemed not to have answered her prayer, she heard a voice say, "Ask for sanctification." She realized she had not actually remembered to ask God to sanctify her! She then prayed a short prayer and immediately received the gift of perfect love. She jumped to her feet and cried, "The Lord has sanctified my soul!"[4] This experience had a lasting impact on Lee's life and her persistence in her calling to preach the gospel.

Phoebe Palmer was the most influential advocate who called Methodism to return to holiness in the mid-nineteenth century. Holiness and entire sanctification were central themes of Palmer's writing and speaking. Some see Palmer's articulation of a "shorter way" as an adaptation and even perhaps a corruption of Wesley's original understanding. It is uncontroversial that she was a crucial figure in bringing the doctrine back into prominence in American Methodism. Her ministry was energized by her own experience of receiving entire sanctification, which she then offered to countless Methodists in the second half of the nineteenth century. She discussed her own experience in a variety of contexts. In one, she simply described rejoicing in "the assurance that I was wholly sanctified—throughout *body, soul,* and *spirit.*"[5]

Leonidas Hamline (1797–1865) was roughly a contemporary of Phoebe Palmer's. He was also the twenty-seventh bishop in the Methodist Episcopal Church. Believe it or not, it was common for Methodist bishops in the nineteenth century to have experienced entire sanctification. Hamline was certainly not the only bishop with a story similar to this one.

Hamline's experience of entire sanctification was preceded by a feeling that God's hand searched inside and outside of him and seemed to leave a clear sense of God's healing and cleansing presence everywhere he felt the hand move. Hamline summarized the experience by saying that he felt as though "God's love swallowed me up."

This was such a powerful experience that Hamline actually "fell to the floor" and "cried out in a loud voice."[6] Hamline's testimony is a reminder that Methodists often encountered God in dramatic and life-changing ways. Methodists were more hungry for holiness than they were worried about being embarrassed in front of others. They were more desperate for God than they were determined to protect their reputations. This also illustrates that such physical responses were more common among Methodists and there was less reason for self-consciousness about them.

And these experiences are found in virtually every season of Methodist vitality. Hester Ann Rogers (1756–1794) had an encounter with God that was ecstatic and dramatic in many ways that predict Hamline's experience. Rogers felt the presence of God "penetrate" her in a way that seemed to lock up her body for a period of time. She was insensible to anything going on around her. All she knew was God's work in her soul.

And then she heard Jesus say to her, "All that I have is thine!" And everything changed for her in a moment. She was so overwhelmed by the power and presence of Christ that she sank down to the ground. She recalled that she was "unable to sustain the weight of his glorious presence and fullness of love."[7] This is an experience that many Pentecostals, charismatics, and other Methodists have had throughout our history—even today.

When God's loving and healing presence is made manifest in someone's life it can lead to a powerful bodily response. People sometimes fall down. People sometimes cry out. When you think about it, this should not be all that surprising. We are talking about being made perfect in love by the power of God. This is a powerful and life-changing experience. It is not surprising that it might be accompanied by a powerful encounter with God that is expressed in physical and embodied ways.

Of course, these kinds of encounters with God need not always be physically demonstrative. The point is the encounter with the Lord and not an experience for its own sake. There are a host of powerful experiences of being made perfect in love that were less dramatic as far as outward signs, but were just as life-changing for the recipient.

Joseph Benson, an early Methodist preacher, provides one example. Benson described his soul being "satiated" with God's goodness. His faith was increased so that all doubt and fear were "banished." And Benson found that he was so filled with love that he was able to surrender everything, every part of his life, to God.

Though Benson's testimony does not include dramatic manifestations of the Spirit upon him that caused him to fall down under the power of God or to cry out, he did experience a deep outpouring of God's love and power. This experience enabled him to devote every part of his life to loving and serving God. Benson testified that he was "put in possession of a new nature" that enabled him to dedicate his life entirely to God. Benson's long life of service to Methodism was confirmation of the impact the ongoing blessing of being "satiated" with God's presence had on his life.[8]

A Doctrine Preached and Experienced through Preaching

Because entire sanctification was the central goal of Methodism, Methodists pursued it with urgency. In the early days of Methodism, entire sanctification was one of the central themes of Methodist preaching and teaching. One example of this is a manuscript sermon from Freeborn Garrettson (1752–1827), an early American Methodist preacher. In his sermon, Garrettson noted that Christians often mistakenly believe that having faith in Jesus and experiencing forgiveness of their sins meant that "the work is complete." If new Christians were "faithful to the grace given," they would eventually realize that there was more work that needed to be done in their souls—a "deeper work." Garrettson saw the recognition of the need for a deeper work after justification and pardon to itself be evidence of the work of the Holy Spirit in one's life. The goal was for Christians to realize that God wants to bring them entirely into alignment with the Spirit's will for their lives.[9]

Garrettson emphasized in his sermon that entire sanctification is by faith, just as justification is by faith in Christ. When someone receives the gift of faith, the Christian grows from immature faith toward mature faith. The Christian, as they grow in maturity, is governed in new and deeper ways by the grace of God.

John Wesley often preached on entire sanctification. He also regularly published sermons that modeled what he did and did not mean by entire sanctification or Christian perfection (see appendices for two such sermons). Methodists often experienced entire sanctification as a result of hearing sermons preached on being made perfect in love.

Jane Cooper wrote to John Wesley in 1761 after she heard him preach on Galatians 5:5: "For we through the Spirit wait for the hope of righteousness by faith" (KJV). The sermon served as a wake-up call to Cooper, as it convicted her of her need for sanctification and the reality that she had not yet experienced it. It also awakened a hunger in her for holiness and to be satisfied in Christ and Christ alone.

After the sermon, Cooper received prayer by another Methodist woman, identified as "Mrs. G." When Mrs. G. prayed for Cooper, she "found salvation by simple faith." Like Joseph Benson's testimony, Cooper did not recount any dramatic physical experience.

She simply received a powerful inner assurance that she had found what she was looking for. She had a strong and intimate sense of Jesus' presence and she knew that Jesus "was mine."

Cooper then described the results of the work that Jesus had done in her life. She found that Jesus "now reigns in my heart without a rival." What a beautiful expression of what we are seeking! Cooper also testified that through faith in Christ's sanctifying work, she found deep and lasting happiness. She wrote simply, "I am happy in God this moment, and I believe for the next."[10]

Contagious Testimony

When Methodists experienced the work of God in their souls, they were expected to give voice to it by testifying to what God had done for them. These testimonies often increased other people's faith and expectation that God would do a similar work for them. Accounts of God's work in the lives of Methodists were often contagious, seeming to spread throughout a gathering.

A great example of this is from Benjamin Abbott (1732–1796), a first-generation American Methodist preacher. Abbott took a break from the annual conference and went off by himself to smoke his pipe. He later testified that as he was smoking, "the Spirit of the Lord came upon me in a miraculous powerful manner so that I was fully convinced that something great would be done at the conference."

In those days, conferences ended with a love feast, which was a time of sharing a simple meal and testifying to how God had moved during the conference. Abbott testified to the experience he had at the love feast. When he told them about his own sanctification, one of the preachers went down. Abbott recounted that preacher "did not rise until the Lord sanctified his soul." Despite the excitement of the first preacher going down, Abbott continued to share his testimony and press people to "claim the promises" of entire sanctification.[11] As Abbott continued speaking, the congregation became more and more animated. People began to go among those who were in distress to minister to them in the ways that they needed. By the end of the love feast, six people told Abbott that they had received entire sanctification! And seven people told him that they had received justification by faith. The Spirit of God had fallen in such a strong way that at the end of the evening, three people had to be carried home, as they were unable to get home on their own.

Testimonies to entire sanctification that exploded into mini-revivals were normal in early Methodism. They were expected in some sense, because all Methodists were encouraged to earnestly pursue entire sanctification. Methodist preachers were required to affirm not only their belief in entire sanctification, but that they were earnestly pursuing and seeking it themselves.

Testimonies to Persistence

Methodists would typically testify to receiving entire sanctification as soon as they received the gift of full salvation and the confirmation of the witness of the Spirit that they had been made perfect in love. As we have seen, these testimonies were often powerful and even contagious, as they helped increase other people's faith and expectation for entire sanctification in their own lives.

Methodists also often testified to their initial experience of entire sanctification in their spiritual autobiographies in ways that expressed their initial experience of Christian perfection and also that God's faithfulness enabled them to continue to walk in perfect love.

Reverend William Bramwell (1759–1818), for example, described his experience of entire sanctification consisting of his soul being "all wonder, love, and praise." Bramwell looked back on this experience twenty-six years later and he was able to testify that he continued to walk in the "liberty" of entire sanctification. He also continued to testify to his experience of entire sanctification every chance he got. Bramwell was adamant that "God does not impart blessings to his children to be concealed in their own bosoms, but to be made known."[12]

Doctor F. G. Hibbard (1811–1895), who was named after the early American Methodist preacher Freeborn Garrettson previously mentioned, received entire sanctification while on a walk on a beautiful spring day. God led Hibbard into entire sanctification through a series of questions to which he realized the answers were all yes! As he walked, Hibbard asked God for "victory over all known sin." And as soon as he asked, he realized he had received this victory. He then asked for "power to perform all the known will of God." Again, he found that his prayer was answered as soon as he asked. Finally, he asked for power to "love God with all my soul." And, again, he found God immediately gave him this power. Hibbard found that from that moment on he never "doubted for one moment the reality of the work there attested."[13]

New Testimonies in a New Day

In recent years, testimonies to receiving entire sanctification are rare. I have met some people who have such a testimony, but the lack of embracing God's gift to Methodism in recent decades has led to a decline in experience of this doctrine. In some parts of contemporary Methodism, there is even an assumption that testifying to entire sanctification would only be something a person who is exceedingly arrogant would be capable of doing.

But this is a misunderstanding of Methodism's gift. Entire sanctification is not a sign that one is an elite or super-spiritual Christian. Rather, it comes as a response to awareness of great need for God to do in us what we cannot do in ourselves. In my experience, people who seek entire sanctification are actually *more aware* of their propensity to sin and *more humble* than people who are not earnestly pursuing full salvation and are more content or apathetic in their Christian walk. Pursuing holiness tends to confront you with your need for holiness, which is humbling and sometimes even painful. And yet, our history reminds us that those who ask do receive and those who seek do find (Luke 11:9–10). And what they find is a priceless treasure.

And yet, the painful truth is that testimonies to entire sanctification have become exceedingly uncommon in contemporary Methodism. What happened? Before we begin to more thoroughly define what Wesley did and did not mean by entire sanctification, we need to understand a bit more about what happened to our grand depositum in our own history.

Small Group Discussion Guide

Open with a Prayer

Questions for Discussion

1. What did it feel like to read the testimonies to entire sanctification throughout this chapter? How are these testimonies similar or different from the ways that you hear people talk about their faith in your community?
2. How do you think people in your church would respond to a sermon preaching and inviting people to receive the gift of entire sanctification? Do you think people are ready? If not, what do you think are the main obstacles to their being ready to receive the gift of perfect love?
3. Have you been in a situation where someone shared a powerful experience with God, and it impacted other people in a way that seemed to be contagious? If so, do you remember the details of the experience? What was shared? Why do you think the testimonies shared in this chapter often led to other people experiencing entire sanctification?

Are you earnestly striving after perfection in love?

How do the testimonies you read this week impact your desire to "earnestly strive after perfection in love"? Do they touch your heart or energize your spirit?

Close with a Prayer

4

What Happened?

What Has Happened to Methodism?

My guess is that some of you reading this have been wondering: What happened to Methodism? What I have been describing may feel really different from your experience of Methodism. How did we get from John Wesley insisting that entire sanctification was the "grand depositum" that God had entrusted to Methodism to a time when very few Methodists have even heard of it?

It's complicated.

Sometime around the middle of the nineteenth century, Methodism began to experience diverging understandings of its core unifying commitments. Over the second half of the nineteenth century, these different understandings continued to move farther and farther apart.

One part of the story is that Methodists like Phoebe Palmer (1807–1874) and B. T. Roberts (1823–1893) began to worry that

Methodism was moving away from its commitment to holiness and entire sanctification. They began to passionately advocate for renewed commitment to holiness and entire sanctification in American Methodism. Part of their passion for seeing Methodism recommit to its grand depositum came from their own experiences of receiving this blessing.

We glimpsed part of Palmer's testimony in the previous chapter. Roberts, who became the key founder of the Free Methodist Church, described his experience in 1865, many years after the fact. Roberts attended a camp meeting in 1849 where "the subject of holiness received special attention." Phoebe Palmer, Roberts specifically noted, was present at the meeting "and labored for the promotion of holiness with great zeal and success." A conviction had been growing in Roberts that his ministry as a Methodist preacher could go in one of two directions. He could "be a popular preacher, gain applause, do but little good in reality, and at last lose my soul." This, obviously, was not the path that he wanted to take, although he did feel drawn to the allure of popularity and worldly success. The other path he saw was one where he would choose to "take the narrow way, declare the whole truth as it is in Jesus, meet with persecution and opposition, but see a thorough work of grace go on, and gain Heaven."

As Roberts saw these two paths before him, he felt that he was brought to a moment of decision. Roberts testified that "Grace was given to make the better choice." He rededicated his life to God and committed "to declare the whole truth as it is in Jesus, and to take the narrow way." Once Roberts made this commitment, the Holy Spirit fell upon him "in an overwhelming degree." This experience was not only a spiritual blessing, it also empowered his work in a way he "had never possessed before." Like many testimonies we saw in the previous chapter, Roberts was also given grace to persist in this experience. His mind had been made up that he would "obey the Lord and take the narrow way, come what will."[1] This experience formed the foundation of the rest of Roberts's ministry, especially his willingness to take an unpopular stand for holiness in the Methodist Episcopal Church which eventually led to his expulsion from the church.[2]

In 1867, a camp meeting (a large-scale revival) was convened in Vineland, New Jersey, with particular focus on the doctrine of holiness. The camp meeting was so successful that at the close of the meeting, key leaders formed a new organization to continue the work, the National Camp Meeting Association for the Promotion of Holiness. The next year a holiness camp meeting in Manheim, Pennsylvania, was attended by an estimated twenty-five thousand people.

As the Holiness Movement grew, it led some to become more insistent on the importance of a return to a stronger emphasis on the doctrine of entire sanctification in the main branches of American Methodism. While many agreed with the need for a return to old-school Methodism, there were other Methodists who were more interested in pursuing new directions in theology coming out of the rise of German Liberal Protestantism as well as a desire to pursue a more culturally influential and economically affluent version of Methodism.

The tensions and disagreements that arose in Methodism in the mid- to late-1800s over the doctrine of entire sanctification led to the rise of several new denominations. The Free Methodist Church, for example, was formed in 1860 after B. T. Roberts and other Methodists in the Genesee Conference were expelled for "unchristian and immoral conduct" due to their persistent advocacy for "old school" Methodism, particularly the doctrine of holiness and the practical expression of it.[3]

As emphasis on the doctrine of entire sanctification waned, some Methodists left to start new denominations dedicated to holiness. Other Methodists were convicted that it was important to stay within the Methodist Episcopal Church and advocate for a return to holiness. Over time it became more and more challenging for those most passionate about holiness to stay within the main branch of Methodism.

Because of the divisions and new denominations that arose related to holiness, a debate emerged within Methodism over whether entire sanctification was, in fact, Wesleyan. Historian Melvin Dieter wrote, "critics of the revival often had charged that the preaching of Christian perfection which became characteristic of the revival was un-Wesleyan because the context of American revivalism tended to create significant variations from Methodism's standard teachings of the doctrine."[4]

Ultimately, it was recognized that commitment to holiness in the first generation of English and American Methodism was so clear and pervasive that arguments that suggested entire sanctification were not Wesleyan failed to persuade. The holiness movement was "so closely identified with traditional Methodism and Wesleyan doctrine and life that Methodist opponents of the revival were forced to distance themselves from Wesley and the standard authors of prevailing Methodist theology to resolve the struggle with the holiness elements within the church."[5]

Opponents of holiness in Methodism eventually conceded that the doctrine was Wesleyan. Those who persisted in opposing the Holiness Movement responded by turning away from Wesley and increasingly looked to Liberal Protestantism for guidance and inspiration.

As a result, instead of looking back to their heritage and tradition, Methodists in the main branch of Methodism increasingly looked forward "to the new and greener pastures in more modern teachers and theologies."[6] Dieter described the transition from Methodism's holiness heritage to Liberal Protestantism in parts of the Methodist family:

> The legacy of entire sanctification, with whatever modifications may have been made to it during the course of the American deeper life revival, was now being surrendered, in large part, to the holiness movement; it had become difficult for the tradition to survive within its original Methodist Episcopal Church and Methodist Episcopal Church South home.[7]

Methodists who were most concerned about cultural respectability increasingly wanted to distance themselves from those they saw as uncultured and fanatical in their pursuit of holiness. As respectable Methodism was forced to choose between their spiritual heritage and growth in wealth, members, and cultural influence, the main branch that would eventually become the United Methodist Church chose the path of worldly power and influence and abandoned their spiritual heritage to the holiness denominations.

The more Wesley's heirs distanced themselves from preaching and teaching their grand depositum, the more they also experienced decline—both spiritually and numerically.

Hope for Retrieving This Today

Some reading this might be wondering: *Is it even realistic that we could retrieve it today*?

My answer is a resounding yes! I am very optimistic that we can return to our theological roots. Although this doctrine has been neglected, it is like an archeological treasure ready to be retrieved.

Entire sanctification already persists in contemporary Methodism in two main places. First, in many Methodist denominations, as people take their vows in the ordination process, they are asked before their colleagues in ministry and, more important, before God, whether they believe in this central teaching and are pursuing it in their own lives with God. Those to be ordained are asked these historic questions: Are you going on to perfection? Do you expect to be made perfect in love in this life? Are you earnestly striving after it?[8]

The expected answer to each of these questions is: "Yes, by the grace of God."

The very fact that for two-and-a-half centuries every ordained clergyperson in virtually all churches connected to the Wesleyan theological heritage have declared their belief in this doctrine before God and their peers represents a powerful latent deposit on the foundation upon which the church has been built.

There are many Methodist clergy who want to experience the best of their heritage.

Second, entire sanctification continues to be a part of the formal doctrine of many denominations that trace their heritage back to John Wesley. (See appendix E for a variety of statements on sanctification.) Here is one example from *The Book of Discipline of The United Methodist Church*:

> We believe sanctification is the work of God's grace through the Word and the Spirit, by which those who have been born again are cleansed from sin in their thoughts, words and acts, and are enabled to live in accordance with God's will, and to strive for holiness without which no one will see the Lord.
>
> Entire sanctification is a state of perfect love, righteousness and true holiness which every regenerate believer may obtain by being delivered from the power of sin, by loving God with all the heart, soul, mind and strength, and by loving one's neighbor as one's self. Through faith in Jesus Christ this gracious gift may be received in this life both gradually and instantaneously, and should be sought earnestly by every child of God.
>
> We believe this experience does not deliver us from the infirmities, ignorance, and mistakes common to man, nor from the possibilities of further sin. The Christian must continue on guard against spiritual pride and seek to gain victory over every temptation to sin. He must respond wholly to the will of God so that sin will lose its power over him; and the world, the flesh, and the devil are put under his feet. Thus he rules over these enemies with watchfulness through the power of the Holy Spirit.[9]

This is a powerful statement! And if you are United Methodist, it is *already* part of your church's formal beliefs. Your church currently teaches that, by the power of God's grace, those in Christ can be "cleansed from sin in their thoughts, words and acts, and are enabled to live in accordance with God's will."

I can't wait to hear a new wave of Methodists today testify to receiving this indescribable gift in their lives! At one level, we simply need to proclaim what we already believe.

All of Wesley's heirs should know about this teaching, not only those who went to seminary. It should be preached in every pulpit, as the result of every pastor's wrestling with what Wesley did and did not mean by perfection, and their efforts to present this to their parishioners in a way that they can understand.

The Bible tells the truth about the human condition. Over and over again, God's people are found to be faithless and disobedient. No matter how many times we try to show God, or ourselves, that we have what it takes, we are found to be wanting. We are confronted by the words of Scripture that "all have sinned and fall short of the glory of God" (Rom. 3:23).

We are not able.

But there is *one* who is able: God the Father, Son, and Holy Spirit!

John Wesley insisted that Methodists cling to the doctrine of entire sanctification because he was convinced that it was true. And he was convinced that God had given Methodists a special mission to preach and teach this doctrine, this audacious optimism that God's grace not only pardons and forgives, but radically transforms. He was convinced that the good life—the life for which Jesus gave his life so that we might live—comes not through self-help, willpower, or trying harder in our own strength.

Rather, the good life, the blessed life, comes through surrender. It comes through telling the truth about our weakness, our desperation, and our great need. When the people of

God get desperate enough and determined enough to experience the kind of life that God intends for us to live, God seems to delight in breaking through and bringing a seemingly impossible blessing.

At the heart of the gospel (which means "good news") is this truth:

> But he said to me, "My grace is sufficient for you, for my power is made perfect in weakness." Therefore I will boast all the more gladly about my weaknesses, so that Christ's power may rest on me. That is why, for Christ's sake, I delight in weaknesses, in insults, in hardships, in persecutions, in difficulties. For when I am weak, then I am strong. (2 Cor. 12:9–10)

Strength comes through admitting our weakness. This is at the heart of the very logic of Christianity. The life, death, and resurrection of Jesus are God's gracious response to our deep need to be saved.

One reason that some are critical of boldly reclaiming entire sanctification in contemporary Methodism is because there are so few testimonies to entire sanctification in the present. When I teach about entire sanctification, someone will inevitably ask me: "Do you actually know anyone who has been entirely sanctified?"

As I said in the previous chapter, I do know people who have been entirely sanctified, though not many. I fully expect, however, to see more people testifying to receiving the gift of being made perfect in love in this life in the near future. I am hearing of more and more people earnestly groaning after full salvation. I have faith that the Holy Spirit will empower Methodists to reclaim our grand depositum once again.

I yearn to hear Methodist preachers encourage the faithful to, like Paul, "press on toward the goal to win the prize for which God has called me heavenward in Christ Jesus" (Phil. 3:14).

It is time to raise the expectations in our churches for what God is able to do in us and through us! Who among us will set their minds on settling for nothing less than persisting in prayer and all of the means of grace until they receive that holiness without which "no one will see the Lord" (Heb. 12:14)?

It is time for a decision. It is time to commit ourselves to a full retrieval of the doctrine of entire sanctification, God's gift to Methodism.

I am convinced John Wesley was right. Proclaiming the audacious optimism of what God's grace can do in the lives of every single person was at the very center of God's purpose for Methodism and all who have followed in Wesley's footsteps. And I do not believe that this doctrine has somehow become irrelevant or obsolete. On the contrary! It is as desperately needed today as it has ever been.

We don't have to look very far to see people living lives of desperation; people with addictions, sexual deception and brokenness, pridefulness and materialism, anger and abusiveness, loneliness and fear. Time and time again, Methodists have taken on the sin, brokenness, and hopelessness around them and embraced the "ministry of reconciliation" (2 Cor. 5:18), whereby lost sinners are restored to fullness of life.

The world desperately needs a people that passionately embraces and winsomely proclaims entire sanctification. And the second half of this book will help us do just that.

Small Group Discussion Guide

Open with a Prayer

Questions for Discussion

1. How does your experience in your congregation compare with the shifts in emphasis on holiness and entire sanctification discussed in this chapter? Where are the places you see room for improvement? What gives you the most hope and optimism for the future?
2. What do you think would be the first steps that would need to be taken in order for the doctrine of entire sanctification to be able to be retrieved both in belief and experience in your own church?
3. Do you agree that a likely reason that contemporary Methodism does not have more testimonies to entire sanctification is because the doctrine has not been taught and that people have not been encouraged to seek it in their own lives? If so, how can this best be addressed?

Are you earnestly striving after perfection in love?

Each group member should take a few minutes to briefly take stock of how they are personally feeling about entire sanctification and their own faith journey. Are you feeling more interested and desirous of seeking greater holiness and even full salvation? Elaborate a bit if you can, one way or the other.

Close with a Prayer

5

Entire Sanctification—What It Is

If I am right that entire sanctification is *still* the grand depositum that God has lodged with the people called Methodists, then we need to know what it is. And we need to reclaim this teaching in every single part of our lives together as Methodists.

This chapter and the next will outline in detail what Wesley did, and did not, mean by entire sanctification. The seventh chapter will outline the extent to which holiness and entire sanctification are grounded in the teaching of Scripture. And the final chapter will discuss how to best pursue entire sanctification today. So, what, exactly, did Wesley mean by entire sanctification?

What Is Entire Sanctification?

John Wesley argued for and preached on entire sanctification throughout his ministry. He understood holiness as "religion itself" and described Methodism as consisting of "only plain scriptural religion, guarded by a few prudential regulations. The essence of it is holiness of heart and life."[1] From the founder of Methodism's perspective, the purpose of the Christian life is to become holy.

Before we can understand entire sanctification, we need a basic definition of sanctification itself. Wesley used holiness and sanctification as synonyms. He offered a definition of sanctification in his sermon "The Scripture Way of Salvation":

> At the same time that we are justified, yea, in that very moment, *sanctification* begins. In that instant we are "born again", "born from above", "born of the Spirit". There is a *real* as well as a *relative* change. We are inwardly renewed by the power of God. We feel the "love of God shed abroad in our heart by the Holy Ghost which is given unto us," producing love to all mankind, and more especially to the children of God; expelling the love of the world, the love of pleasure, of ease, of honour, of money; together with pride, anger, self-will, and every other evil temper—in a word, changing the "earthly, sensual, devilish" mind into "the mind which was in Christ Jesus."[2]

Holiness, then, involves God's work to change us from the inside out. God gives us a new heart and new affections. As we become holy, we come to love God and what God loves more and more over time. Becoming holy also entails a transfer of allegiance from the carnal fleshly things of this world (love of the world, pleasure, comfort, fame, pride, and so forth) to the things of God.

Growth in holiness or sanctification, as well as Christian perfection, are by faith, just as justification is by faith. Wesley described the faith by which Christians are entirely sanctified as expressed in terms of four specific beliefs, each building on the previous: (1) God has promised this in Scripture; (2) What God promises, God is able to do; (3) God is able and willing to do it now; and (4) God actually does this.[3]

Wesley's most succinct definition of entire sanctification was "love excluding sin."[4] At its most basic level, one who has received entire sanctification no longer sins because they have been captivated by the love of God. In his sermon "Christian Perfection," Wesley was quick to acknowledge that many doubt whether this is really possible for the children of God. He was adamant that the question should be decided not "by abstract reasonings" or "the experience of this or that particular person." Wesley insisted that the question be decided solely based on the witness of Scripture. To this end, he cited Romans 6:

> What shall we say, then? Shall we go on sinning so that grace may increase? By no means! We are those who have died to sin; how can we live in it any longer? Or don't you know that all of us who were baptized into Christ Jesus were baptized into his death? We were therefore buried with him through baptism into death in order that, just as Christ was raised from the dead through the glory of the Father, we too may live a new life.
>
> For if we have been united with him in a death like his, we will certainly also be united with him in a resurrection like his. For we know that our old self was crucified with him so that the body ruled by sin might be done away with, that we should no longer be slaves to sin—because anyone who has died has been set free from sin.
>
> Now if we died with Christ, we believe that we will also live with him. For we know that since Christ was raised from the dead, he cannot die again; death no longer

has mastery over him. The death he died, he died to sin once for all; but the life he lives, he lives to God.

In the same way, count yourselves dead to sin but alive to God in Christ Jesus. Therefore do not let sin reign in your mortal body so that you obey its evil desires. Do not offer any part of yourself to sin as an instrument of wickedness, but rather offer yourselves to God as those who have been brought from death to life; and offer every part of yourself to him as an instrument of righteousness. For sin shall no longer be your master, because you are not under the law, but under grace.

What then? Shall we sin because we are not under the law but under grace? By no means! Don't you know that when you offer yourselves to someone as obedient slaves, you are slaves of the one you obey—whether you are slaves to sin, which leads to death, or to obedience, which leads to righteousness? But thanks be to God that, though you used to be slaves to sin, you have come to obey from your heart the pattern of teaching that has now claimed your allegiance. You have been set free from sin and have become slaves to righteousness.

I am using an example from everyday life because of your human limitations. Just as you used to offer yourselves as slaves to impurity and to ever-increasing wickedness, so now offer yourselves as slaves to righteousness leading to holiness. When you were slaves to sin, you were free from the control of righteousness. What benefit did you reap at that time from the things you are now ashamed of? Those things result in death! But now that you have been set free from sin and have become slaves of God, the benefit you

> reap leads to holiness, and the result is eternal life. For the wages of sin is death, but the gift of God is eternal life in Christ Jesus our Lord.

The most surprising (and humbling!) part of Wesley's sermon to a Methodist who has not read it may be his assertion that "all real Christians or believers in Christ, are made free from outward sin." Wesley's high expectations for all Christians, not only those who have experienced entire sanctification, comes from his reading of the Bible. First John 3:9, for example, reads: "No one who is born of God will continue to sin, because God's seed remains in them; they cannot go on sinning, because they have been born of God." This verse combined with the previous verse ("the one who does what is sinful is of the devil") sets up a strong contrast between one who is born of God and one who is born of the devil.

Wesley spent significant time in his sermon "Christian Perfection" addressing the argument made by some that Christians do, at least sometimes, commit outward sin. He was immovably opposed to this argument and refused to concede this point. Wesley insisted that a new era and new possibility and empowerment had been unleashed through the work of Jesus Christ, the only Son of God. Because of the work of Christ, those who put their faith in Christ are no longer *servants* of God, but are *sons and daughters* of God. (See, for example, Galatians 3:23–4:7.) And so, Wesley doubled down on 1 John: "We know that anyone born of God does not continue to sin; the One who was born of God keeps them safe, and the evil one cannot harm them" (5:18).

Wesley refused to concede that it was necessary for the apostles to sin, or that if they did sin it would mean that it is necessary that we sin now: "No necessity of sinning was laid upon *them*. The grace of God was surely sufficient for them. And it *is* sufficient for *us* at this day."[5] He goes on to cite 1 Corinthians 10:13, which reads in part: "God is faithful; he will not let you be tempted beyond what you can bear. But when you are tempted, he will also provide a way out so that you can endure it."

Wesley addressed many other arguments he encountered for why outward sin is a necessary part of the Christian life. He argued against each one and returned to his original statement about Christian perfection: "A Christian is so far perfect as not to commit sin."[6] Wesley's biblically grounded conviction that any Christian, even a brand-new Christian, is able to resist outward sin may be the place where Methodism's expectation for the Christian life has drifted the farthest from its beginnings and its theological heritage.

If a Christian does not commit outward sin, what makes entire sanctification different?

One who has experienced Christian perfection is "freed from evil thoughts and evil tempers."[7] Wesley's logic here is that one who has experienced Christian perfection has been given a clean heart that loves God to the exclusion of sin. As a result, evil thoughts no longer come from a clean and sanctified heart. He argues in favor of entirely sanctified Christians being freed from evil tempers by building on the words of Jesus in Matthew 10:24: "The student is not above the teacher, nor a servant above his master." Jesus "was free from all sinful tempers. So therefore is his disciple, even every real Christian."[8]

Another key passage of Scripture for Wesley regarding the impact of Christian perfection on the recipient is Galatians 2:20: "I have been crucified with Christ and I no longer live, but Christ lives in me. The life I now live in the body, I live by faith in the Son of God, who loved me and gave himself for me." Wesley sees this verse as describing a "deliverance from inward as well as from outward sin."[9]

More specifically, Wesley taught that entire sanctification brings a purification of heart by faith, referencing Acts 15:9, which reads in part: "he purified their hearts by faith." The heart is specifically purified from pride and anger. Wesley does qualify the extent to which one is purified from anger, as even Jesus was angry at times. (See, for example, Mark 3:5.) One who is entirely sanctified may be angry at sins that are committed, while grieving for the people who commit those sins. One can be angry at sin and offences against God, but the one who has experienced Christian perfection will feel "only love and tender compassion to the offender."[10] Most of us do not have to think very hard to see the difference between anger at sin and anger, even hatred, toward those who sin against us. This is, indeed, a radical change.

A response that Wesley commonly encountered to his understanding of entire sanctification was that Jesus saves us from these kinds of sins, but not until death. Wesley disagreed with the idea that growth in holiness had to be gradualistic and like a destination one got closer to, but never really arrived. He specifically wanted to know how a gradualistic view of Christians receiving the promises of God was reconciled with the witness of Scripture. In contrast to such a view, he cited 1 John 4:17: "This is how love is made complete among us so that we will have confidence on the day of judgment: *In this world we are like Jesus*" (italics mine). The King James Version of the Bible, the translation Wesley would have read, particularly highlights Wesley's conviction: "Herein is our *love made perfect*, that we may have boldness in the day of judgment: because *as he is, so are we in this world*" (italics mine).

In order to make sure his audience didn't miss the point he was making, Wesley offered his own interpretation of 1 John 4:17: "The Apostle here beyond all contradiction speaks of himself and other living Christians, of whom (as though he had foreseen this very evasion, and set himself to overturn it from the foundation) he flatly affirms that not only at or after death but 'in this world' they are as their Master."[11]

The most controversial part of Wesley's understanding of Christian perfection is actually not really the doctrine of Christian perfection itself. It is the step before it. Wesley argued that all Christians no longer commit outward sin. He was adamant that anyone who has come to faith in Jesus and has experienced justification by faith (forgiveness or pardon from past sins) and the new birth (regeneration) does not actively do things that they know are contrary to God's will. This is a stark contrast to the expectations of most churches today. We are offered an opportunity to repent and turn fully to the Lord Jesus Christ and his will for our lives.

Wesley reminded us to look to the witness of Scripture. He cited passages like 2 Corinthians 7:1: "Therefore, since we have these promises, dear friends, let us purify ourselves from everything that contaminates body and spirit, perfecting holiness out of reverence for God."

Summary

We have covered a lot of ground so far. Let's conclude this part by summarizing Wesley's understanding of our grand depositum of entire sanctification. Toward the end of his sermon "Christian

Perfection," Wesley offered a fairly straightforward definition: "Christians are saved in this world from all sin, from all unrighteousness; that they are now in such a sense perfect as not to commit sin, and to be freed from evil thoughts and evil tempers."[12] Again, because of his claim that all Christians no longer commit outward sin, the distinction of entire sanctification is really that Christians receive additional freedom from evil thoughts and evil tempers.

In his sermon "The Scripture Way of Salvation," perhaps Wesley's best-known sermon, he defines entire sanctification as:

> A full salvation from all our sins, from pride, self-will, anger, unbelief, or, as the Apostle expresses it, "Go on to perfection" [Heb. 6:1 KJV]. But what is perfection? The word has various senses: here it means *perfect love*. It is *love excluding sin*; love filling the heart, *taking up the whole capacity of the soul*. It is love "rejoicing evermore, praying without ceasing, in everything giving thanks" [1 Thess. 5:16–18 KJV].[13]

Wesley here describes Christian perfection, or entire sanctification, as "perfect love." Sin is excluded from perfect love. The two cannot exist together. Sanctification is entire in that the love of God "fills the heart" and "takes up the whole capacity of the soul." Perfect love leads to constant rejoicing, prayer, and thanksgiving.

The ability to fight sin and be victorious over its power is good news and dramatically underemphasized in the contemporary church. In fact, this victory, according to John Wesley, actually occurs with justification and regeneration. And so, entire sanctification is *more than* the ability not to sin.

Entire sanctification is not simply negative—just not sinning. Every Christian, according to Wesley, is free from the power of sin! Entire sanctification is a deeper work: rooting out what Wesley called the "root" or "being" of sin. How? By the love of God filling the heart. This is true freedom, not simply guilt and power, but from its very being.

Here is Wesley's concluding exhortation to pursue perfect love in his sermon "Christian Perfection." Notice that his appeal is soaked with the words of Scripture:

> "Having therefore these promises, dearly beloved," both in the Law and in the Prophets, and having the prophetic word confirmed unto us in the Gospel, by our blessed Lord and his apostles; "let us cleanse ourselves from all filthiness of flesh and spirit, perfecting holiness in the fear of God" [2 Cor. 7:1]. "Let us fear, lest" so many "promises being made us of entering into his rest," which he that has entered into, has ceased from his own works, "any of us should come short of it" [Heb. 4:1]. "This one thing let us do, forgetting those things which are behind, and reaching forth unto those things which are before, let us press toward the mark, for the prize of the high calling of God in Christ Jesus" [Phil. 3:13–14]; crying unto him day and night, till we also are "delivered from the bondage of corruption, into the glorious liberty of the sons of God!" [Rom. 8:21].

Let us raise our expectations so that they are in sync with the promises of Scripture! May we refuse to settle for less than the full salvation offered to us through the gospel.

Small Group Discussion Guide

Open with a Prayer

Questions for Discussion

1. How would you describe holiness or sanctification based on what you read in this chapter?
2. Imagine trying to explain this concept to someone outside of your group. How would you explain to this person Methodism's conviction that entire sanctification is necessary and good news? And how would you define the doctrine? Take some time together as a group to come up with the best answer you could give to each of these.
3. What did you find to be most challenging to you or hardest to embrace in this chapter? Were there passages from Scripture that were connected to this place that helped you to see the warrant in Scripture for this teaching? If so, does that help? What is the most compelling answer you can come up with in answer to your own question?

Are you earnestly striving after perfection in love?

We are getting closer to a point of decision. You now have quite a bit of background information about the doctrine of entire sanctification and its role in early Methodism, changes in American Methodism, and Wesley's understanding of this doctrine. This week I want to invite you to take another step into deeper water with your group and simply answer the question as honestly as you are able to: Are you earnestly striving after perfection in love?

Close with a Prayer

6

Entire Sanctification—What It Isn't

Of all of the doctrines taught by John Wesley and his first followers, Christian perfection was both the most misunderstood and the most controversial. This was evident to Wesley early on in the Methodist movement.

Because of the extent of controversy and confusion, Wesley spent significant time and energy clarifying what he did and did not mean by Christian perfection. Wesley's sermon "Christian Perfection" was written to limit the misunderstanding and misuse of the doctrine. (You can read the sermon in its entirety in appendix B.) He dedicated the first half of the sermon to a discussion of what is *not* meant by Christian perfection. These clarifications are crucial to avoiding common misunderstandings of Methodism's grand depositum.

What Is Not Meant by Entire Sanctification?

The sermon began by acknowledging that the doctrine has caused offence, especially the word *perfect*. Many recommended that Wesley simply abandon the phrase because of the misunderstanding and controversy that it seemed inevitably to attract. Wesley refused, asking "are they not found in the oracles of God [Scriptures]? If so, by what authority can any messenger of God lay them aside, even though all men should be offended?"[1]

Among other passages of Scripture, Wesley would have had Matthew 5:48 in mind: "Be perfect, therefore, as your heavenly Father is perfect." Wesley was adamant that passages of Scripture cannot be laid aside because they are difficult or challenging to our own sense of what is reasonable or possible to expect from ourselves or others. He was equally insistent, however, that the meaning of Scripture be understood as fully and accurately as possible "that those who are sincere of heart may not err to the right hand or to the left from the mark of the prize of their high calling."[2]

Here are five specific things Wesley says are *not* meant by Christian perfection:

They are not perfect in knowledge or free from ignorance.

Those who experience Christian perfection may have similar knowledge "in common with other men, many things relating to the present world."[3] They may also be ignorant of many things which are largely irrelevant to Christian faith and discipleship, such as particular matters of science, history, or various areas of technical expertise. One can have experienced Christian perfection, for example, and not know how to change a tire or be able to name the presidents of the United States of America in order.

Rather than focusing on knowledge of things in this world, Wesley focused more on the things that a Christian *does* know. They know the love of God in a personal way and that they are children of God. They know the power and presence of the Holy Spirit in a direct and immediate way. And they know "the wisdom of his providence directing all their paths, and causing all things to work together for their good."[4] And perhaps most important for Wesley's understanding of Christian perfection, "They know in every circumstance of life what the Lord requireth of them, and how 'to keep a conscience void of offence both toward God and toward man.'"[5]

Wesley also allowed significant room for mystery in the Christian life. Christians are not perfect in knowledge of theology. Here, Wesley was not calling core doctrines like the doctrine of the Trinity into question. Far from it! Rather, he acknowledged that divine revelation contains inexhaustible riches that we rightly seek to understand, though the mysteries of God are, at times, beyond rational comprehension.

Wesley particularly emphasized that Christians who have experienced entire sanctification do not know when Christ will return in glory, ushering in the new creation. At first glance, it may seem unnecessary to explicitly state that those who are entirely sanctified will not have access to special revelation about the return of Christ. It did, however, prove to be a necessary clarification in Wesley's lifetime as George Bell, an early Methodist lay preacher, began to make increasingly extravagant claims after professing to have been made perfect in love. The final straw for

Wesley came when Bell prophesied that the world was going to end on February 28, 1763.

Spoiler alert: it didn't.

Wesley was quick to counter Bell's prophecy. On the day that Bell predicted that the world would end, Wesley preached on Amos 4:12: "Prepare to meet thy God" (KJV). Using this passage, Wesley "showed the utter absurdity of the supposition that the world was to end that night." Despite his sermon, many people were afraid to go to sleep that night; "some wandered about in the fields, being persuaded that if the world did not end, at least London would be swallowed up by an earthquake." For his part, Wesley recorded in his *Journal*: "I went to bed at my usual time and was fast asleep about ten o'clock."[6]

Wesley also conceded that those who have experienced Christian perfection do not necessarily understand God's work in their own lives. They may not understand why something has happened to them or to someone they love. They may never fully understand in this life why some things have happened, or other things have not happened. God does, at times, graciously answer our frequent desire to know why, but not always. For Christians who tend to see significance or symbolism in every random occurrence in their lives, it may be helpful to remember that even those who have experienced Christian perfection do not always understand the ways that God has worked in their own lives.

They are not free from mistakes.

If one who has experienced Christian perfection does not know everything, they will likely make mistakes due to their own ignorance. There are a variety of ways in which someone may fall short that Wesley would not consider to be sinning or demonstrating that one has not been entirely sanctified. A person who has been entirely sanctified can forget things. They may also make a variety of other mistakes. Someone who is entirely sanctified, for example, could make a poor measurement that leads to a piece of wood being cut too short. Or, they could make a mistake in doing a math problem. Or, they could accidentally knock over a fragile and precious heirloom, causing it to be irreparably damaged.

This qualification of entire sanctification may initially seem obvious and unnecessary. However, one of the most common pushbacks against Christian perfection is typically that it is not possible for people to be perfect in this life. The concern often seems to be a perfection of performance along the lines previously mentioned. Methodism's grand depositum is *not* an unhealthy perfectionism, where people are condemned for making mistakes. Rather, entire sanctification is a *freedom from* and *power over* willfully violating God's commands that comes from being filled with the love of God in Christ.

Wesley says that "the children of God do not mistake as to the things essential to salvation . . . But in things unessential to salvation they do err, and that frequently."[7] This is an important qualification. Though Christians will make mistakes, Wesley is insisting that there are essential beliefs and practices that one who is entirely sanctified both understands and lives out. If this were not the case, the concept itself would lose all meaning and significance. Nevertheless, Wesley also allows that there may even be disagreement among the children of God regarding the "interpretation of many places in Holy Writ." And yet, even here, he seems to exclude diverging readings of Scripture that are related to Christian practice, or Christian ethics. Wesley was passionately committed to Methodists pursuing holiness together, which required agreement on the concrete realities of how one lives their life.

They are not free from infirmities.

Those who experience Christian perfection are not immune to getting sick. This has been a source of misunderstanding in some parts of Christianity. If a Christian gets cancer, that does *not* invalidate the maturity of their faith or the depth of their commitment to Jesus. Those who have experienced full salvation will still be subject to the same frailties in this world as anyone else. They may get head colds or the flu. They may be in serious accidents, or be diagnosed with a terminal illness. Until Christ returns in glory, everyone who is born will die at some point. And only God knows when that will happen.

Christians should not blame people who get sick for their illness. It is appropriate for Christians to pray for the sick to be healed. However, if someone is not healed, they should never be told that they were not healed because they did not have enough faith.

Wesley also understands infirmities to be a broader category than physical illness. He includes "weakness or slowness of understanding, dullness or confusedness of apprehension, incoherency of thought, irregular quickness or heaviness of imagination."[8] Here, Wesley is making allowance for a variety of mental mistakes and a range of normal human emotions.

While he does not directly address this, Wesley's thinking here also prevents entire sanctification from being reserved for a kind of intellectual elite. Entire sanctification is not only for people with a high enough IQ or the right academic degrees. Because entire sanctification is simply a gift of God that comes through faith in the work of Christ, it is not only for people of a certain intellectual ability. And one is not disqualified from receiving God's perfect love by an infirmity.

They are not wholly free from temptation.

Those who experience Christian perfection are not entirely free from temptation. One can be walking in perfect love for God and neighbor and experience temptation to do something that would clearly be sin. One, however, cannot indulge that temptation or give in to it. God's grace gives Christians a new freedom to resist sin and patterns of sinning rather than submit to the inevitability of it.

This is a crucial pastoral concession. Most people—if not, all people—have a particular place or a few places where they are particularly prone to wander or fall into a habitual sin. When you practice or repeat the same sin regularly, it becomes easier and easier to repeat that sin. It also becomes more and more difficult to resist the temptation to sin when it first arises. Addiction may be the easiest way to illustrate this. Someone who has become addicted to drugs, alcohol, or pornography will find it easier to fall again, despite their increased disgust at the sin and at themselves for another failure and their determination to not go there.

By the grace of God, people who are addicted in a particular way can find freedom from their addiction. I previously mentioned my friend who was instantly delivered from a decades-long addiction to chewing tobacco. In his experience, the desire for chewing tobacco was simply taken from him. He went forward for prayer at a worship service (for something else!) and soon afterward noticed that he just didn't have any desire for the stuff anymore. It is wonderful when God wins a victory on our behalf in such a complete and effortless way!

But this is also not how God seems to work with most people. Many people who struggle with addiction, or any besetting sin, find God winning a victory on their behalf where their power to fight against that addiction is restored to them, but they also still find that there are times when they feel a draw to give themselves to that sin again. This is why it is not a good idea for recovering alcoholics to hang out in bars or why people who are recovering from addiction to pornography need to have clear boundaries and accountability around their use of screens.

All of this is to say that a person who is entirely sanctified will no longer submit to these old habits of sin. But they may feel the pull of these old ways on their hearts and souls. The key is that they now consistently find, as Wesley would have read in the King James Version of the Bible: "Ye are of God, little children, and have overcome them: because greater is he that is in you, than he that is in the world" (1 John 4:4). One who is entirely sanctified experiences a new depth of power over sin and restoration of their will so that they can once again exercise their will to choose obedience and faithfulness to God over the ways of sin and death.

They are not free from the need for further growth.

Finally, there is not any "absolute perfection on earth."[9] A person who experiences entire sanctification is still on a journey. They still need to grow daily in grace. Dr. Doug M. Strong, one of my seminary professors and mentors, described entire sanctification as "giving all that I know of myself to all that I know of God." The giving is complete. Nothing is withheld. But I will know more about God the more I continue to rely upon the means of grace like reading Scripture, praying, and worshiping with disciplined commitment. And I will know more about myself the more I learn and grow and gain life experience. And so, over time, I am able to give more of myself to the God I am coming to know more.

This means that entire sanctification is itself an experience to grow in. When we receive this gift, we are still desperately dependent on the grace of God. We must continue to practice the basics of the Christian faith, just like an elite athlete continues to practice the fundamentals of their sport. Entire sanctification is a new level of freedom from sin's power in one's life. But it is more like finding a new level of strength and power for living a faithful Christian life than crossing a finish line or arriving at a final destination. Those who receive entire sanctification by the grace of God continue to be on a journey following Jesus Christ their Lord and Savior.

Here is what is at stake: no matter how much you have grown in your faith, no matter how completely you have given yourself to God, you still need to "grow in grace" (2 Peter 3:18) and "daily advance in the knowledge and love of God his Saviour."[10]

May it be so!

Can Someone Who Has Been Entirely Sanctified Ever Sin Again?

There is one other aspect of entire sanctification that has been misunderstood at times and may have done more to discredit entire sanctification than anything else. It is this point: Can someone who has received the gift of entire sanctification sin again?

The short answer is yes.

Methodists believe that someone who has had a genuine experience of justification by faith and is currently in right relationship with God can cease cooperating with God's grace and intentionally turn away from God. A person can regress at any point in the Christian life. Sadly, and its most extreme, this can even happen to the point of someone completely renouncing their faith and losing their salvation entirely.

The Wesleyan understanding of Christian discipleship is dynamic at every stage. There is always room to grow and move forward in our relationship with God. And there is also the possibility of moving away from God, which has often been referred to as "backsliding" by Methodists.

People who experience entire sanctification can still sin. The key distinction is that the power of sin in their lives has been uprooted and they have been graciously empowered by God with the ability to perfectly love God and neighbor. A person who experiences entire sanctification is entirely sanctified as long as they continue to cooperate with God's grace and walk in the freedom they have received.

So, what happens if someone who has experienced entire sanctification does sin?

There is always hope. A person who sins after experiencing entire sanctification needs to do the same thing that any Christian who falls into sin needs to do: confess their sin and repent. This hope for forgiveness and pardon is grounded in Scripture:

> My dear children, I write this to you so that you will not sin. But if anybody does sin, we have an advocate with the

> Father—Jesus Christ, the Righteous One. He is the atoning sacrifice for our sins, and not only for ours but also for the sins of the whole world. (1 John 2:1–2)

We may fall short (though we do not need to) even after receiving the precious gift of entire sanctification. But Jesus is always faithful. His promises never change.

One of the challenges with the doctrine of entire sanctification in the past has been that some people who have made public professions of entire sanctification backslid but denied it. It was obvious to their community that they had fallen, but they weren't able or willing to confess and repent. This has led to legalism in some communities that have embraced entire sanctification. The focus tends to be on an external list of sinful behaviors to be avoided, while sometimes the affections and matters of the heart are ignored.

Remember that entire sanctification is, above all else, about receiving God's perfect love so that we can love God and each other entirely.

Encouraging the pursuit of entire sanctification and embracing the experience when God gives it can be challenging for a variety of reasons. My sense is that a church that embodies Methodism's grand depositum will have many people who have testimonies to entire sanctification. Some will have persisted in this freedom to love God and others to the exclusion of sin for decades. And the church should praise God for these living witnesses! There will also be people who got a glimpse of this experience and walked in complete freedom for a season, but backslid. The church should rejoice in the freedom they experienced and hold the hope of Scriptures like 1 John 2:1–2.

My hope would be that the church that embraces entire sanctification would help people tell the truth about where they are in their life and in their relationship with God and others. And that the church would encourage each other to keep moving forward, even if in order to move forward we have to acknowledge where we have fallen short.

This seems more complicated when talking about entire sanctification because we are talking about a person who has had an especially powerful experience of God's grace.

The challenge is to take sin and its devastating consequences seriously and hold up the promise and possibility of freedom from sin's grip on our lives on the one hand, while also resisting the pull toward legalism or hypocrisy on the other hand.

Only by the grace of God can we walk this fine line. But the good news is Scripture clearly and repeatedly speaks to God's desire to do a great work in us.

Small Group Discussion Guide

Open with a Prayer

Questions for Discussion

1. Did this chapter help you better understand what Wesley meant by entire sanctification or Christian perfection? Which limitation on his understanding of entire sanctification had the biggest impact on making this doctrine more credible to you?
2. Of the things that Wesley said are not included in Christian perfection, which do you think is the most common mistake that people make today in their expectations of mature Christian living for themselves or for others?
3. The end of the chapter reinforces that entire sanctification is an experience in which we continue to grow and not a static end point. How does knowing that entire sanctification is an experience that still includes ongoing growth and development, even after it is experienced, impact the way that you think about this doctrine?

Are you earnestly striving after perfection in love?

Take time again for each group member to check in and give their answer to this question. If it helps you answer the question, you might think about the impact that studying this specific teaching has had on your faith overall.

Close with a Prayer

7

Grounded in Scripture

Entire Sanctification Is Biblical

Wesley began his main treatise on the doctrine of Christian perfection by discussing the early influences on his thinking. He wrote that, in 1725, at the age of twenty-three, he read Jeremy Taylor's *The Rule and Exercises of Holy Living and Dying*, which convinced him of the need for "purity of intention" in his faith in Christ. In 1726, he read Thomas à Kempis's *The Imitation of Christ*, which showed him "the nature and extent of inward religion" and the need to give "all my heart" to God. And a few years later he read William Law's *Christian Perfection* and *A Serious Call to a Devout and Holy Life*. These books, Wesley recounted, "convinced me, more than ever, of the absolute impossibility of being half a Christian; and I determined, through his grace . . . to be all-devoted to God, to give him all my soul, my body, and my substance."[1]

Though there were multiple influences on his thinking, the most important influence on Wesley was Scripture. Wesley recounts that in 1729 he began "not only to read, but to study, the Bible, as the one, the only standard of truth, and the only model of pure religion." From this study of the Bible he "saw, in a clearer and clearer light, the indispensable necessity of having 'the mind which was in Christ,' and of 'walking as Christ also walked.'"[2] Wesley's commitment to prayer and searching the Scriptures is well known. One of the main ways that Wesley communicated his core theological convictions to Methodists throughout his life was by writing sermons that expounded on key aspects of Scripture and the Christian life. Wesley's orienting concern was salvation. He wanted to know what salvation was and how people experience salvation. And he was certain that the best guide to salvation was Scripture itself.

In the preface to his collection of sermons, he made clear his commitment to the central role of Scripture and his focus on teaching the way of salvation. One of the best-known passages in Wesley's writings comes from this preface:

> I want to know one thing, the way to heaven—how to land safe on that happy shore. God himself has condescended to teach the way: for this very end he came from heaven. He hath written it down in a book. O give me that book! At any price give me the Book of God! I have it. Here is knowledge enough for me. Let me be *homo unius libri* [a man of one book]. Here then I am, far from the busy ways of men. I sit down alone: only God is here. In his presence I open, I read his Book; for this end, to find the way to heaven.[3]

It is fitting that this passage ends with a repeat of Wesley's desire to know "the way to heaven." He expected to find out how to find reconciliation and peace with God through the witness of Scripture. And he wanted to share what he had learned for the good of others.

Wesley was convinced that the best way to teach the "Scripture Way of Salvation," which was the title of one of his sermons, was through sermons. These allowed him to start with a Scripture passage and then work through its implications for finding the way to heaven. Wesley gave further insight into his own intentions in doing this in the same preface:

> I have accordingly set down in the following sermons what I find in the Bible concerning the way to heaven, with a view to distinguish this way of God from all those which are the inventions of men. I have endeavoured to describe the true, the scriptural, experimental religion, so as to omit nothing which is a real part thereof, and to add nothing thereto which is not. And herein it is more especially my desire, first, to guard those who are just setting their faces toward heaven (and who, having little acquaintance with the things of God, are the more liable to be turned out of the way) from formality, from mere outside religion, which has almost driven heart-religion out of the world; and secondly, to warn those who know the religion of the heart, the faith which worketh by love, lest at any time they make void the law through faith, and so fall back into the snare of the devil.[4]

The more that Wesley studied the Bible, the more convinced he became that holiness of heart and life was a central theme of Scripture, and that it was, in fact, the focus of the Christian life itself. Wesley outlined this in a particularly memorable way in one of his most succinct summaries of Methodist doctrine: "Our main doctrines, which include all the rest, are three, that of repentance, of faith, and of holiness. The first of these we account . . . the porch of religion; the next, the door; the third is religion itself."[5]

The goal of Methodism was to help people turn away from sin (repentance), turn to Jesus Christ (faith), and then to become a deeply committed follower of Jesus Christ (holiness). If you begin reading Scripture looking for the emphasis on holiness, you will notice that the concern for holiness soaks the Bible's pages from Genesis through Revelation.

In hopes of helping you see this a bit more quickly, here are a few of the key passages related to Scripture's emphasis on sanctification. What follows is neither exhaustive nor comprehensive. My hope is to give you a head start in seeing just how prevalent the message of holiness is throughout Scripture, though I have left out many passages I would have liked to include (especially regarding the Old Testament) due to space constraints.

It is important to start by being clear that the Bible is concerned with holiness in both the Old and New Testaments. The Bible is a story of God's plan to save the nations by working through a particular people (Abraham, Isaac, and Jacob and their descendants) and a particular person (Jesus). The first five books of the Bible are the story of God's covenant with Israel and the ways in which he has called them and set them apart for their sake and for the sake of all people. The call to holiness is seen in many places. It is seen with particular clarity in Leviticus. Here are two examples:

> "I am the LORD your God; consecrate yourselves and be holy, because I am holy. Do not make yourselves unclean by any creature that moves along the ground. I am the LORD, who brought you up out of Egypt to be your God; therefore be holy, because I am holy." (11:44–45)

> "You are to be holy to me because I, the LORD, am holy, and I have set you apart from the nations to be my own." (20:26)

Holiness, then, is being set apart by God. There are many examples of things being consecrated or set apart as holy to God. In Exodus 39:30, for example, a plate made for the tabernacle is set apart with a seal: "They made the plate, the sacred emblem, out of pure gold and engraved on it, like an inscription on a seal: HOLY TO THE LORD."

God is holy. And God's holiness serves as a call to worship the Lord. There are many such examples in Psalms. One is found in Psalm 99:

> The LORD reigns,
>   let the nations tremble;
> he sits enthroned between the cherubim,
>   let the earth shake.
> Great is the LORD in Zion;
>   he is exalted over all the nations.
> Let them praise your great and awesome name—
>   he is holy.
>
> The King is mighty, he loves justice—
>   you have established equity;
> in Jacob you have done
>   what is just and right.

Exalt the Lord our God
    and worship at his footstool;
    he is holy.

Moses and Aaron were among his priests,
    Samuel was among those who called on his name;
they called on the Lord
    and he answered them.
He spoke to them from the pillar of cloud;
    they kept his statutes and the decrees he gave them.
Lord our God,
    you answered them;
you were to Israel a forgiving God,
    though you punished their misdeeds.
Exalt the Lord our God
    and worship on his holy mountain,
for the Lord our God is holy.

Isaiah, in a beautiful passage describing the joy of the redeemed, discusses the highway of holiness:

And a highway will be there;
    it will be called the Way of Holiness;
    it will be for those who walk on that Way.
The unclean will not journey on it;
    wicked fools will not go about on it.
No lion will be there,
    nor any ravenous beast;
    they will not be found there.
But only the redeemed will walk there,
    and those the Lord has rescued will return.

They will enter Zion with singing;
    everlasting joy will crown their heads.
Gladness and joy will overtake them,
    and sorrow and sighing will flee away. (Isa. 35:8–10)

In the New Testament, the Gospels tell the good news of the life, death, and resurrection of Jesus Christ. Throughout Jesus' ministry in the Gospels, the story is told to demonstrate that Jesus is more than a good example for us to follow. Jesus is the very *logos* (word or logic) of God made flesh. Jesus is God in human form. He is fully human and fully God.

Jesus is at the center of the Christian understanding of salvation. Jesus makes forgiveness and pardon with God for sin possible. We can approach God the Father with confidence that we will receive what we do not deserve (grace, forgiveness, and healing) because of the work that Jesus has done for us. Jesus makes it possible for us to not only be forgiven, but also to be empowered to live lives of joyful obedience and faithfulness to God.

In the Gospel of John, Jesus spoke directly to his desires for us and his work for our sanctification:

> "I am coming to you now, but I say these things while I am still in the world, so that they may have the full measure of my joy within them. I have given them your word and the world has hated them, for they are not of the world any more than I am of the world. My prayer is not that you take them out of the world but that you protect them from the evil one. They are not of the world, even as I am not of it. Sanctify them by the truth; your word is truth. As you sent me into the world, I have sent them into the world. For

> them I sanctify myself, that they too may be truly sanctified." (17:13–19)

In the Sermon on the Mount, Jesus made several strong statements that seem to raise the expectations for those who are following the God of Abraham, Isaac, and Jacob. Somewhere close to the middle of the Sermon on the Mount, Jesus said simply: "Be perfect, therefore, as your heavenly Father is perfect" (Matt. 5:48).

Holiness is also a clear and persistent theme across the rest of the New Testament, just as it is in the Old Testament and the Gospels. First Peter 1:13–16, for example, calls Christians to be "alert" and "fully sober," concluding by citing the passage from Leviticus 11:44–45:

> Therefore, with minds that are alert and fully sober, set your hope on the grace to be brought to you when Jesus Christ is revealed at his coming. As obedient children, do not conform to the evil desires you had when you lived in ignorance. But just as he who called you is holy, so be holy in all you do; for it is written: "Be holy, because I am holy."

Second Peter 1:3–11 (NRSV) begins by affirming that the power of God "has given us everything needed for life and godliness, through the knowledge of him who called us by his own glory and goodness." The passage continues:

> Thus he has given us, through these things, his precious and very great promises, so that through them you may escape from the corruption that is in the world because of lust, and may become participants of the divine nature. For this very reason, you must make every effort to support your faith with goodness, and goodness with knowledge,

> and knowledge with self-control, and self-control with endurance, and endurance with godliness, and godliness with mutual affection, and mutual affection with love. For if these things are yours and are increasing among you, they keep you from being ineffective and unfruitful in the knowledge of our Lord Jesus Christ. For anyone who lacks these things is short-sighted and blind, and is forgetful of the cleansing of past sins. Therefore, brothers and sisters, be all the more eager to confirm your call and election, for if you do this, you will never stumble. For in this way, entry into the eternal kingdom of our Lord and Savior Jesus Christ will be richly provided for you.

The Pauline letters contain multiple passages that both affirm the importance of holiness and eloquently speak to the work that God has done to make sanctification possible. Paul included a call to holiness in the very beginning of the letter to the Ephesians: "Praise be to the God and Father of our Lord Jesus Christ, who has blessed us in the heavenly realms with every spiritual blessing in Christ. For he chose us in him before the creation of the world to be holy and blameless in his sight" (Eph. 1:3–4).

Paul also offered caution in several of his letters about the consequences of remaining in sin. In 1 Corinthians 6:9–11, Paul cautioned the Christians in Corinth that "wrongdoers will not inherit the kingdom of God." He then named a variety of people who do wrong ("the sexually immoral," "idolaters," "adulterers," "men who have sex with men," "greedy," "drunkards," "slanderers," and "swindlers"). Paul was adamant that such people will not "inherit the kingdom of God." And he was aware that some of those reading his letter were exactly those kinds of people. But Paul reminded his audience of the good news of the gospel of Jesus Christ: "But you were washed, you were sanctified, you were justified in the name of the Lord Jesus Christ and by the Spirit of our God."

Paul made a similar statement in Titus 2:11–14, where he again contrasted the way that the grace of God enables us to say no to things that are not of God and also enables us to say yes to God's will:

> For the grace of God has appeared that offers salvation to all people. It teaches us to say "No" to ungodliness and worldly passions, and to live self-controlled, upright and godly lives in this present age, while we wait for the blessed hope—the appearing of the glory of our great God and Savior, Jesus Christ, who gave himself for us to redeem us from all wickedness and to purify for himself a people that are his very own, eager to do what is good.

In 2 Timothy 1:6–14, Paul reminded Timothy to tend to the gift of God that was given to him through the laying on of hands and to be unashamed of the gospel. In this passage, Paul explicitly affirmed that God "has saved us and called us to a holy life . . . because of his own purpose and grace" (v. 9).

> For this reason I remind you to fan into flame the gift of God, which is in you through the laying on of my hands. For the Spirit God gave us does not make us timid, but gives us power, love and self-discipline. So do not be ashamed of the testimony about our Lord or of me his prisoner. Rather, join with me in suffering for the gospel, by the power of God. He has saved us and called us to a holy life—not because of anything we have done but because of his own purpose and grace. This grace was given us in Christ Jesus before

> the beginning of time, but it has not been revealed through the appearing of our Savior, Christ Jesus, who has destroyed death and has brought life and immortality to light through the gospel. And of this gospel I was appointed a herald and an apostle and a teacher. That is why I am suffering as I am. Yet this is not cause for shame, because I know whom I have believed, and am convinced that he is able to guard what I have entrusted to him until that day.
>
> What you heard from me, keep as the pattern of sound teaching, with faith and love in Christ Jesus. Guard the good deposit that was entrusted to you—guard it with the help of the Holy Spirit who lives in us.

In 2 Thessalonians 2:13–17, Paul called on the church in Thessalonica to give thanks that they had been chosen by God "to be saved through the sanctifying work of the Spirit." The passage then exhorts these Christians to "stand firm and hold fast to the teachings we passed on to you."

> But we ought always to thank God for you, brothers and sisters loved by the Lord, because God chose you as firstfruits to be saved through the sanctifying work of the Spirit and through belief in the truth. He called you to this through our gospel, that you might share in the glory of our Lord Jesus Christ.
>
> So then, brothers and sisters, stand firm and hold fast to the teachings we passed on to you, whether by word of mouth or by letter.
>
> May our Lord Jesus Christ himself and God our Father, who loved us and by his grace gave us eternal encouragement and good hope, encourage your hearts and strengthen you in every good deed and word.

Hebrews 9:11–14 discusses sanctification in the context of the sacrificial system in the Old Testament and the way in which the work of Christ replaces that system, bringing cleansing and enabling us to serve God:

> But when Christ came as high priest of the good things that are now already here, he went through the greater and more perfect tabernacle that is not made with human hands, that is to say, is not a part of this creation. He did not enter by means of the blood of goats and calves; but he entered the Most Holy Place once for all by his own blood, thus obtaining eternal redemption. The blood of goats and bulls and the ashes of a heifer sprinkled on those who are ceremonially unclean sanctify them so that they are outwardly clean. How much more, then, will the blood of Christ, who through the eternal Spirit offered himself unblemished to God, cleanse our consciences from acts that lead to death, so that we may serve the living God!

The Johannine Epistles also contain many passages that are crucial to Wesley's understanding of the importance of holiness. First John 1:5–2:6 is one of the best expressions of Wesley's understanding of what is possible in the Christian life:

> This is the message we have heard from him and declare to you: God is light; in him there is no darkness at all. If we claim to have fellowship with him and yet walk in the darkness, we lie and do not live out the truth. But if we walk in the light, as he is in the light, we have fellowship with one another, and the blood of Jesus, his Son, purifies us from all sin.

> If we claim to be without sin, we deceive ourselves and the truth is not in us. If we confess our sins, he is faithful and just and will forgive us our sins and purify us from all unrighteousness. If we claim we have not sinned, we make him out to be a liar and his word is not in us.
>
> My dear children, I write this to you so that you will not sin. But if anybody does sin, we have an advocate with the Father—Jesus Christ, the Righteous One. He is the atoning sacrifice for our sins, and not only for ours but also for the sins of the whole world.
>
> We know that we have come to know him if we keep his commands. Whoever says, "I know him," but does not do what he commands is a liar, and the truth is not in that person. But if anyone obeys his word, love for God is truly made complete in them. This is how we know we are in him: Whoever claims to live in him must live as Jesus did.

First John 3:1–10 outlines the contrast between love of God and love of sin. Children of God receive God's love and are empowered to love God and what God loves. Children of the devil do the devil's works and love sin.

> See what great love the Father has lavished on us, that we should be called children of God! And that is what we are! The reason the world does not know us is that it did not know him. Dear friends, now we are children of God, and what we will be has not yet been made known. But we know that when Christ appears, we shall be like him, for we shall see him as he is. All who have this hope in him purify themselves, just as he is pure.

> Everyone who sins breaks the law; in fact, sin is lawlessness. But you know that he appeared so that he might take away our sins. And in him is no sin. No one who lives in him keeps on sinning. No one who continues to sin has either seen him or known him.
>
> Dear children, do not let anyone lead you astray. The one who does what is right is righteous, just as he is righteous. The one who does what is sinful is of the devil, because the devil has been sinning from the beginning. The reason the Son of God appeared was to destroy the devil's work. No one who is born of God will continue to sin, because God's seed remains in them; they cannot go on sinning, because they have been born of God. This is how we know who the children of God are and who the children of the devil are: Anyone who does not do what is right is not God's child, nor is anyone who does not love their brother and sister.

First John 4:4 also contains a key affirmation for Christians. We are able to experience full salvation in this life "because the one who is in you is greater than the one who is in the world."

"It Is God's Will That You Should Be Sanctified"

I want to close this brief tour of the Bible's call to holiness and entire sanctification with two passages from 1 Thessalonians that point to Scripture's witness to this doctrine with particular clarity.

> As for other matters, brothers and sisters, we instructed you how to live in order to please God, as in fact you are living. Now we ask you and urge you in the Lord Jesus to do this more and more. For you know what instructions we gave you by the authority of the Lord Jesus.
>
> It is God's will that you should be sanctified: that you should avoid sexual immorality; that each of you should learn to control your own body in a way that is holy and honorable, not in passionate lust like the pagans, who do not know God; and that in this matter no one should wrong or take advantage of a brother or sister. The Lord will punish all those who commit such sins, as we told you and warned you before. For God did not call us to be impure, but to live a holy life. Therefore, anyone who rejects this instruction does not reject a human being but God, the very God who gives you his Holy Spirit. (4:1–8)

In this passage, Paul asserted explicitly that "it is God's will that you should be sanctified." He then listed ways in which this growth in holiness will be expressed. There is a sober warning that God "will punish all those who commit [the previously named] sins, as we told you and warned you before." The call to "live a holy life," according to Paul, is from God and those who reject this call reject not Paul or any other person, but "the very God who gives you his Holy Spirit."

At the end of the next chapter, Paul returned to the kind of life that leads to growth in holiness. He then reiterated the call to pursue entire sanctification:

> Rejoice always, pray continually, give thanks in all circumstances; for this is God's will for you in Christ Jesus.
>
> Do not quench the Spirit. Do not treat prophecies with contempt but test them all; hold on to what is good, reject every kind of evil.
>
> May God himself, the God of peace, sanctify you through and through. May your whole spirit, soul and body be kept blameless at the coming of our Lord Jesus Christ. The one who calls you is faithful, and he will do it. (5:16–24)

When read together, these passages from 1 Thessalonians reveal that sanctification is God's will. It is God's purpose for those who take on the name of Jesus Christ and call themselves Christians. The passage concludes with not only an expression that this is God's will, but a promise that God will be faithful in enabling us to receive what he wills. The New Revised Standard Version translates 5:23–24 in a way that makes this even more clear: "May the God of peace himself *sanctify you entirely*; and may your spirit and soul and body be kept sound and blameless at the coming of our Lord Jesus Christ. The one who calls you is faithful, and *he will do this*" (italics added).

This was the source of Wesley's burden to exhort Methodists to pursue the fullness of salvation. He called Methodists to entire sanctification because he read in Scripture that this was God's will for Christians. And he further read not only that this was God's will, but that God promised to actually do this.

As Wesley read Scripture, he became more and more convinced that entire sanctification was something that God wanted to do and actually did. As he would put it in his sermon "The Scripture Way of Salvation," we ought to expect God to entirely sanctify us by faith (because it is promised in Scripture), as we are (because it is not about works righteousness or us earning it), and now. Wesley intentionally placed urgency on expecting to receive entire sanctification now. If God is ready and willing to do this in us, what are we waiting for?

And now we are ready to consider how we can best put ourselves in a position to receive this great gift!

Small Group Discussion Guide

Open with a Prayer

Questions for Discussion

1. How have the passages of Scripture presented in this chapter challenged or informed your understanding of the goal of the Christian life?
2. Was there a passage of Scripture that was most surprising to you or you felt like you had missed and not quite noticed in your previous reading and study of the Bible?
3. Do you think that the Bible supports Methodism's understanding of holiness and entire sanctification? Why or why not?

Are you earnestly striving after perfection in love?

Each member should be given an opportunity to discuss the extent to which they have been earnest in their pursuit of entire sanctification over the past week.

Close with a Prayer

8

How to Receive Entire Sanctification Today

Entire Sanctification Is a Journey with Others

The importance of small group formation has already been mentioned, but it needs to be reinforced here. Small groups like the band meeting were essential to the early Methodist pursuit of entire sanctification. I don't think it would be an exaggeration to say that Wesley would have thought it very unlikely for someone to retain their experience of entire sanctification if they were not actively participating in a group like the band meeting.

Let me be blunt. You are highly unlikely to experience entire sanctification on your own. Methodism is built on the assumption that we need each other in order to reach our goal. We need others to watch over us and help us see what we cannot see by ourselves. We need people who, like Aaron and Hur did for Moses in Exodus 17:12, will hold up our hands when we grow weary—who will support and encourage us. We need people we know love us, so we can hear them when they challenge us.

If you are serious about receiving entire sanctification, you need to gather together with a group of like-minded followers of Jesus.[1]

Okay, so, hopefully, you have committed to gather together with fellow believers to seek entire sanctification in earnest. This next part may feel like a jarring shift. It is something of a paradox. You need to pursue entire sanctification with expectation that God will give it to you in a moment. This is to say that the pursuit of entire sanctification is both a process by which we continually seek further growth in grace, no matter how much we've grown, and a breakthrough of God's grace we look for every moment, just like our experience of justification by faith and new birth. In his sermon "The Scripture Way of Salvation," Wesley broke this down into three simple steps.

Seek It by Faith

We have not understood the pursuit of holiness until we have gotten crystal clear that holiness is a work that God does for us and in us and not a work that we do for God. And this is very good news if we think about our own experience, right? Have you ever tried to do better at something that you felt like you were failing at? How did that go for you? In some areas, thankfully, we make real progress. But we also know from experience how often our own strength is not sufficient. Too many people are not experiencing the freedom from sin and the inward transformation that comes through faith in Christ. Perhaps you have experienced the sting of regret after losing your patience with your children.

Or maybe you have experienced the feelings of shame that come on the other side of giving in to a sexual temptation. You struggled with hating yourself for having done it. And you promised that you would never, ever do that again. And then you did it . . . again.

Or maybe you have struggled with eating or drinking too much in order to comfort or soothe yourself when things are stressful and challenging in your life. After eating or drinking far more than was necessary you feel disgusting, or you are aware you crossed the boundary from having a drink into drunkenness.

Or, maybe it is shopping.

The list, unfortunately, could go on. In many respects, we do not sin in very creative ways. One of the reasons Wesley encouraged Methodists to be in a group like the band meeting was that telling the truth about failure and struggle to real people often helps remove the feelings of shame and isolation, or the lie no one could ever love you if they really knew you. And often in these contexts, people discover that the places where they have struggled are the same places where other people have struggled as well.

Just like justification and the new birth, sanctification and even entire sanctification are by faith and not by works. This is good news, because if entire sanctification were achieved by works, the doctrine would be a constant source of frustration, falling short and missing the mark. It would be bad news because we would be called to a standard that we were not capable of living up to. Just as we can't free ourselves from sin's power, we can't pour God's love out so that it fills our heart.

So, if we are not able to entirely sanctify ourselves, what is our hope?

Our hope is not in our power. It is in the power of the living God. Let's quickly review the core of the gospel: The Father sent his Son into the world to save the world. The Son lived a life of perfect obedience and submission to the will of the Father. The world was incapable of recognizing the gift that had been sent. Jesus was beaten, tortured, and killed. But God's determination to seek and to save the lost was so great that even the crucifixion of Jesus, his literal death, could not conquer or destroy God's determination to seek and to save the lost. So the Spirit is poured out on all flesh, and we are made adopted children of God. As Peter put it, "For you have been born again, not of perishable seed, but of imperishable, through the living and enduring word of God" (1 Peter 1:23).

The doctrine of justification by faith is one of the best-known doctrines of the Protestant Reformation. We are justified, or pardoned, not by our merit or works, but through faith in the work of Jesus Christ. As Paul continued in Romans, "Therefore, since we have been justified through faith, we have peace with God through our Lord Jesus Christ" (5:1).

The possibility, indeed, the necessity of sanctification, or growth in holiness after justification, has been less well-known in Protestantism—though it has been emphasized by the founding theologians across Protestantism from Luther and Calvin to Wesley.

The first step to receiving entire sanctification is simply seeking it by faith, just as you sought justification by faith. This means sanctification is not first about *you* doing something. It is about trust and confidence that God has promised to give this gift to you and being ready and willing to receive it.

We Seek It as We Are

If entire sanctification is sought by faith, and not by our own works or our own goodness, then it follows that we seek it as we are, not as we think we ought to be. Remember that entire sanctification is about God doing in us that which we cannot do for ourselves.

When you think of holiness, what are the obstacles that immediately come to the front of your mind? Where are the places that you feel most stuck, or where does it feel most preposterous to you that you could win not just one skirmish, but the entire war?

These are exactly the areas where we need to press in and ask God to do in us what we cannot do in ourselves. Don't let your own discouragement, fear, or shame hold you back. We ought to begin by admitting that it is impossible for us to win this war in our own strength. We are not the source of perfect love. God is.

But if we have a clear-eyed view of the gospel, our lack of holiness shouldn't discourage us. Wesley, when discussing this aspect of entire sanctification, would often cite Matthew 19:26: "Jesus looked at them and said, 'With man this is impossible, but with God all things are possible.'"

The doctrine of entire sanctification really stands or falls on whether God wills for us to be made holy. And we have already seen that this is exactly what Scripture teaches according to 1 Thessalonians 4:3: "It is God's will that you should be sanctified."

The logic of entire sanctification is that God is able to accomplish what God intends to accomplish. The resistance to or outright rejection of entire sanctification often focuses on the doctrine being impractical or too unrealistic about what people are able to accomplish. But again, this is not a work that we do for God. If Christianity were about what we were able to do, we would all be lost!

Does God intend to make us perfect in love? Wesley thought Deuteronomy 30:6 made his case: "The LORD your God will circumcise your hearts and the hearts of your descendants, so that you may love him with all your heart and with all your soul, and live." Another important passage of Scripture to this end is Hebrews 12:14: "Make every effort to live in peace with everyone and to be holy; without holiness no one will see the Lord." Wesley understood passages like this and Matthew 5:48—"Be perfect, therefore, as your heavenly Father is perfect"—to be promises that are covered by God.

At first glance, they seem to be impossible commands. But God would not require something of us that is impossible. These passages of Scripture point to a promise of what God intends to accomplish through our cooperation.

Seek entire sanctification by faith. And because we receive entire sanctification by faith, we seek it as we are, not after we think we have sufficiently gotten our acts together. As Wesley said in "Scripture Way of Salvation," "Do *you* believe we are sanctified by faith? Be true then to your principle; and look for this blessing just as you are, neither better nor worse; as a poor sinner that has still nothing to pay, nothing to plead, but 'Christ died.'"

We Seek It Now!

Finally, if entire sanctification is by faith and as we are, Wesley exhorted us to seek it *now*! Toward the end of the sermon "The Scripture Way of Salvation," Wesley urged his audience to seek entire sanctification now, with urgency and expectation:

> [Entire sanctification is] a divine evidence and conviction that he is able and willing to do it *now*. And why not? Is not a moment to him the same as a thousand years? He cannot want more time to accomplish whatever is his will. And he cannot want or stay for any more *worthiness* of *fitness* in the persons he is pleased to honour. We may therefore boldly say, at any point of time, "Now is the day of salvation." "*Today* if ye will hear his voice, harden not your hearts." "Behold! all things are now ready! Come unto the marriage!"[2]

Wesley's logic was that if God wants to do something, he is able to do it now. What could require God to wait? God is not like us. He does not need time to prepare or work toward a goal. He is perfect and exists outside of space and time. He lacks nothing. And so, there is no reason to argue with Paul, who wrote in 2 Corinthians 6:2, "I tell you, now is the time of God's favor, now is the day of salvation."

Wesley then added that there is one more aspect of the faith by which "we are sanctified, saved from sin and perfected in love."[3]

> To this confidence, that God is both able and willing to sanctify us *now*, there needs to be added one thing more, a divine evidence and conviction that *he doth it*. In that hour

> it is done. God says to the inmost soul, "According to thy faith be it unto thee!" Then the soul is pure from every spot of sin; "it is clean from all unrighteousness." The believer then experiences the deep meaning of those solemn words, "If we walk in the light, as he is in the light, we have fellowship one with another, and the blood of Jesus Christ his Son cleanseth us from all sin" [1 John 1:7 KJV].[4]

It is not enough to stop at a theoretical affirmation of entire sanctification, where we say in theory it is possible that God *might* give someone the gift of perfect love now. Wesley pressed farther to affirm that God actually does this. He wants us to be fully engaged and to have *expectant faith.*

Rather than sitting back passively and thinking that God might do that for someone else, but not for us, Wesley wanted everyone to be on the edge of their seats, filled with faith, waiting, hoping, and expecting for God to perfect them in love, sanctify them entirely. Wesley wanted us to be like a kid on Christmas Eve—so excited we cannot sleep, an almost agonizing sense of expectation that we will receive this gift. Can you see how Christmas for a child pales in comparison to the gift of freedom from sin and a heart filled with love?

Can you imagine being so filled with a hunger for holiness that you could not sleep? Can you imagine praying for this gift in the middle of the night because you are so desperate to receive all that God has for you?

Even as I write this, I have faith that the Holy Spirit is giving people such a hunger and thirst for holiness.

I invite you to read the end of "Scripture Way of Salvation" slowly. As you read this passage, seek to be open to the movement of the Holy Spirit. I know that reading something written

250 years ago can be challenging. Please stay with me here. If you read the next paragraph carefully, even repeatedly, until it really sinks in, you will be blessed. Understanding this final passage of "The Scripture Way of Salvation" is essential for grasping the power of the grand depositum that God has given to Methodism. As you read, I believe God will use these words to awaken deeper faith and hunger for full salvation in you.

> "But does God work this great work in the soul *gradually* or *instantaneously*?" Perhaps it may be gradually wrought in some. I mean in this sense—they do not advert to the particular moment wherein sin ceases to be. But it is infinitely desirable, were it the will of God, that it should be done instantaneously; that the Lord should destroy sin "by the breath of his mouth" in a moment, in the twinkling of an eye. And so he generally does, a plain fact of which there is evidence enough to satisfy any unprejudiced person. *Thou* therefore look for it every moment. Look for it in the way above described; in all those "good works" whereunto thou art "created anew in Christ Jesus." There is then no danger. You can be no worse, if you are no better for that expectation. For were you to be disappointed of your hope, still you lose nothing. But you shall not be disappointed of your hope: it will come, and will not tarry. Look for it then every day, every hour, every moment. Why not this hour, this moment? Certainly you may look for it *now*, if you believe it is by faith. And by this token may you surely know whether you seek it by faith or by works. If by works, you want something to be done *first, before* you are sanctified. You think, "I must first *be* or *do* thus or thus." Then you are seeking it by works unto this day. If you seek it by

> faith, you may expect it *as you are*: and if as you are, then expect it *now*. It is of importance to observe that there is an inseparable connection between these three points—expect it *by faith*, expect it *as you are*, and expect it *now*! To deny one of them is to deny them all: to allow one is to allow them all. Do *you* believe we are sanctified by faith? Be true then to your principle, and look for this blessing just as you are, neither better, nor worse; as a poor sinner that has still nothing to pay, nothing to plead but "Christ died." And if you look for it as you are, then expect it *now*. Stay for nothing. Why should you? Christ is ready. And he is all you want. He is waiting for you. He is at the door! Let your inmost soul cry out,
>
> Come in, come in, thou heavenly Guest!
> Nor hence again remove;
> But sup with me, and let the feast
> Be everlasting love.[5]

This is the challenge of entire sanctification. It goes right to the heart of our own desire to be self-sufficient and in control of our lives. When we think about the possibilities for transformation, we most naturally turn inward and think about what we believe is possible by our own strength. But entire sanctification is a direct challenge to our own self-sufficiency.

If entire sanctification were a work for us to do, it would be a cruel and impossible ideal. But like initial salvation, full salvation is a sheer gift of God's grace. God is the one who sanctifies entirely. It is the power of God, not our own power, that is in question when we ask whether entire sanctification is possible.

I love engaging with people who are wrestling with whether this could really be possible, especially in conversation with students. My favorite question to ask after we have talked about entire sanctification from a variety of angles is this one, which I hope you will prayerfully consider: Which is more powerful in the world today, the grace of God or sin?

On this side of the resurrection of Jesus Christ, I do not believe Christians are authorized to say that sin is a necessary or inevitable part of the Christian life. Christ has already defeated the power of sin and even death itself. This defeat has not yet been fully expressed throughout God's creation. But those who are in Christ have access to the power of the resurrection in their own lives.

Remember the words of Scripture from 1 Thessalonians 5:23–24: "May the God of peace himself sanctify you entirely . . . The one who calls you is faithful, and he will do this" (NRSV). What a beautiful promise! Paul prayed for God to entirely sanctify believers so that we will be prepared for the return of Christ. How will entire sanctification happen? *The one who calls you is faithful, and he will do this!*

God does not stir up a yearning in us to "Love the Lord your God with all your heart and with all your soul and with all your mind," or to "Love your neighbor as yourself" (see Matthew 22:37–40) without also giving us the power and the ability to actually love God and neighbor.

God is faithful.

God will finish the work that he has started in us.

Okay, but Really, How Do I Do This?

There is a bit of a tension here. On the one hand, because entire sanctification is a gift that God gives to us, all we can do is receive the gift. We don't make the gift in order to give it to ourselves.

And we can't earn the gift. If the gift is not ours and we can't earn it, but is something that God wants to give to us, we are right to seek it by faith, as we are, and now.

Does this mean that we should do nothing but ask for the gift of entire sanctification and then simply wait for it? No. God may give us the faith to receive the gift of entire sanctification immediately, the very first time we ask for it. And we should ask with the expectation that God will not fail to answer our prayer.

And yet, Wesley taught all Methodists to seek the Lord by daily practicing their faith with discipline and persistence. Many Methodists spent significant time and energy pursuing the gift of entire sanctification. One of the ways that God makes us holy is through giving us a hunger and thirst to persistently pursue holiness. We grow in holiness through disciplined and persistent practice of our faith. The pursuit of God is itself a part of the journey of sanctification. The hunger for holiness is itself a mark of growing in holiness.

One of the consistent themes of John Wesley's ministry is the importance of relying on the means of grace.[6] The means of grace are practices where God's healing and sanctifying presence is reliably experienced. At any point in the Christian life when we are waiting on God to do a work in us, we wait on God by practicing the means of grace. Engaging in these practices is one of the most reliable ways one can grow in holiness.

Wesley argued that the instituted means of grace are a special set of practices that God has wedded himself to. We should give priority of place to these practices in the Christian life because God has committed to always meet with us in these places and because they are instituted by Christ in Scripture.

So, what are these practices?

In Wesley's first attempt at a doctrinal summary for his preachers, he identified the instituted means of grace as:

- Prayer
- Searching the Scriptures
- The Lord's Supper
- Fasting
- Christian Conferencing (which, in Methodism, were the class and band meetings)[7]

These are the key practices of the Christian life. This means that these are the things that people who want to grow in their faith will do.

At one level, this is an easy way to distinguish between our intentions and our actions. It is one thing to say that I want to be a mature and faithful Christian. It is another thing to express that commitment through consistent action. For Wesley, a quick and easy way of gauging whether or not we are serious about putting ourselves in a position to receive the gift of entire sanctification is whether or not we consistently practice the means of grace.

I invite you to take a quick inventory of your life. On a normal day do you spend focused time reading the Bible and in prayer? How often do you fast? Is receiving the Lord's Supper a priority? For Wesley, this is both about receiving Communion as well as about attending public worship. In the Church of England of Wesley's day, the Lord's Supper was a consistent part of Sunday worship. Are you connected to a small group of people who meet regularly and encourage and challenge each other to grow in their faith and to seek the full gospel?

The point of asking these questions is not to shame you or give you a guilt trip. I really mean that! Rather, it is a quick and relatively simple diagnostic for where you are. You need to know where you are in order to know where you have room to grow in your life with Christ.

If you are serious about full salvation, you will want to find ways to commit to these fundamentals of the Christian faith. Wesley (and many others before and after him) was pessimistic about the likelihood of growing in the Christian life without a willingness to show up in the places where God has promised to meet us.

It is also a way of gauging whether or not our intentions are in sync with our actions. If we habitually set aside these practices for other things, then those other things are really our core priorities. They are what are molding and shaping our lives.

Living a life that is firmly grounded in the means of grace may be one of the most difficult and countercultural things that a Christian can do today. We live in persistent and prevalent busyness. Many of us are so addicted to being busy that we are hardly able to recognize it for the sickness that it is, particularly if it is pulling us away from spending intentional and focused time in God's presence.

The importance of the means of grace can be illustrated in a variety of ways. The one that makes the most sense to me is thinking about the importance of practice for expertise. You cannot become an expert at playing baseball, or playing the clarinet, or speaking a foreign language without consistent practice. You cannot make up for a lack of regular practice by cramming. You cannot make up for years of not practicing French by spending one weekend focused solely on French. You can learn a few phrases, but you cannot become fluent in a language by cramming.

So it is with the Christian life.

The joy of practice is that in the game, so to speak, you find that you are able to naturally do things that were previously unnatural.

So it is with the Christian life.

All of this is to say that the most basic thing that you need to do is wait on God to give you the gift of full salvation by practicing the means of grace. We wait actively, not passively.

The means of grace provide the broad context for active waiting. Let me conclude with some more specific thoughts about how to pursue entire sanctification itself:

First, start by regularly reading the passages from Scripture in chapter 7. Ask God to increase your faith as you read these passages. Ask the Lord to increase your faith that these verses speak not merely to abstract or theoretical ideas, but that they speak to what God makes possible for you right now. Ask God to help you look to Jesus and his power and not to yourself and your own sufficiency. Remind yourself that growth in holiness comes through faith or trust and confidence in Jesus, not in yourself. Remind yourself that this is a work that God already wants to do in you. The Lord is ready and willing.

Second, ask the Holy Spirit to show you the way forward. God knows exactly where you are and the Lord knows exactly what you need. God is a good Father who gives good gifts to his children (Matt. 7:11). Ask the Holy Spirit to enable you to trust God with every single part of your life. Ask for power to give all of yourself to God.

I think Wesley had it exactly right. We seek full salvation by faith, as we are, and now. This presses a basic question upon us: Are we currently expecting it right now? If not, why not? Is it because we doubt God's ability to do the work in us? Is it because we are unwilling to be made like Jesus? Do we doubt whether we can really trust our lives completely to God? These are crucial places to wrestle with the Lord in prayer. Be honest.

Finally, I am reminded of Jarena Lee's own testimony (from chapter 3). Don't forget to ask. Ask directly for God to sanctify you entirely. If this is new to you, this may seem like a very strange prayer to pray. You may have to pray it multiple times before God answers it in your own life. If you do, know that you are in good company. Testimonies to entire sanctification in early Methodism nearly always came after a period of earnest and intentional pursuit of the blessing in prayer, sometimes for hours—even throughout the entire night. Some Methodists sought this blessing for months before finding a breakthrough. Ask the Lord to give you the ability to persevere and continue pursuing all that God has for your life, every blessing that Jesus has made available to you.

And don't forget to ask specifically for God to give you the gift of entire sanctification. Here is one simple prayer:

Father, by the power of the Holy Spirit, sanctify me entirely for the sake of your Son, Jesus.

Small Group Discussion Guide

Open with a Prayer

Questions for Discussion

1. What does it mean to you that sanctification and full salvation are by faith alone, just as justification is by faith alone? Is this easy or difficult for you to accept? Why?
2. How does Wesley's insistence that entire sanctification is to be sought as we are change your thinking about your relationship with God and what is possible? Wesley intended this to be received as good news. Does it feel like good news to you? Why or why not?
3. Wesley's conviction that entire sanctification is by faith and not by works led him to insist that we should expect it not only as we are, but *now*. How did this emphasis resonate with you? What would you say your overall eagerness to receive entire sanctification was after you finished this chapter?

Are you earnestly striving after perfection in love?

Each member of the group should take a moment to reflect on the impact that the past eight weeks have had on their pursuit of the full blessing that God has for their life. Has this group impacted your openness and expectation of more intimacy, connection, and love for God and ability to love others? Given Wesley's insistence that we wait for the gift of full salvation actively and not passively, how are you doing in consistently practicing the means of grace? Is there a particular place you have room to grow? Are you earnestly striving after perfection in love?

Close with a Prayer

Epilogue

Hope for Methodism's Future

I want to close this book with a word of hope. I am hopeful because I am convinced that the doctrine of entire sanctification is true. I hope this book has convinced you that it is true too. Entire sanctification is biblical. And it has been experienced, testified to, and witnessed by countless people throughout our history, even if we've overlooked or ignored them of late.

I am hopeful because I believe the Methodist theological tradition is ideally positioned to address the cultural challenges the church is facing. Cultural Christianity characterized by Wesley as the "form of religion without the power" is becoming less and less compelling. I expect to see it die out entirely during my lifetime. And I have come to see this as good news.

Cultural Christianity has meant that the church itself has been double-minded for too long, pulled between loyalty to Jesus and loyalty to cultural influence and acceptance. As the culture abandons any pretense to value Christianity, there will be one reason to belong to the church and call yourself a Christian: you have been found by Jesus Christ, the only Lord and Savior. And people who have been found by Jesus are willing to give all of their lives to him and to learn to follow him as faithfully and completely as they can.

We live in a time where people are desperate for community, belonging, hope, healing, and real transformation. The Methodist theological tradition is ideally positioned to address all of these crucial needs. Methodism is designed to help people connect with a God who is real and who cares about them. We need each other. And we need to connect in deep, vulnerable, and authentic ways. In the age of disembodied ever-present pseudo connections, I'm not sure there has ever been more of a need or hunger for community and connection in person. This is at the core of our DNA.

I am hopeful because God has already given us the answers we need for such a time as this. We just need to rediscover what the Lord has entrusted to us.

If I'm honest, my hope is also connected to a kind of desperation. I hope it is a holy desperation. I have been captivated by the doctrine of entire sanctification since the first time I encountered it. I remember thinking that it put words to what I had sensed about the Christian life but had not been able to articulate since I came to faith when I was in middle school. I have become increasingly desperate to witness a people who really believe what we say we believe.

I yearn to see a body of Christians so captivated by Jesus that they dare trust him for deliverance from everything that keeps them from abundant living. I yearn to connect with Christians who have settled in their hearts and minds that Jesus is the way, the truth, and the life. I need community that shares common vision for living like Jesus in our particular time and place. I am desperate for this kind of church.

I want to see what God does through a group of believers who put Jesus first in their families, their jobs, and everything else. I need to see a community living like this. It is far easier to find examples of half-measures and compromise. I want to see others go all in for Christ and be influenced by them.

I have blind spots. The vision here isn't just a hope for other people, it is something I need myself.

I am yearning for God to raise up, once again, a people who have decided to follow Jesus, no matter what, and no matter the cost. As I wrote this, I found myself thinking about the kind of peace that comes when you make a hard decision, but you have really and truly made the decision. It is often then that peace comes, that rest comes, that you sleep deeply and through the night for the first time in far too long.

This starts with you.

Methodism is desperate for courageous and bold moral leadership. Methodism is desperate for leaders who have settled their minds and hearts on pursuing the holiness without which no one will see the Lord—no matter what. You do not have to be a pastor to lead in this way (though if you are a pastor, I really hope that you will). Methodism needs passionate laity who will not accept anything less than real Methodism from the clergy.

Finally, I hope this book has raised your own hopes and expectations for what God wants to do in your life. One of the things I have tried to avoid throughout my writing is leaving you feeling like I have burdened you with a heavy load and the weight of unhealthy expectation and perfectionism. This is all too common in our culture.

I hope I am leaving you feeling energized, convicted, and excited by new possibilities for your life in Christ, and hungry to experience more of the Spirit's sanctifying power in your life. I hope you have not felt the weight of a heavy burden or guilt settling on your shoulders. That has not been my intention.

In the Gospel of Jesus Christ according to Matthew, Jesus tells us that he brings good news to those who are weary and burdened. He promises rest. If we follow Jesus and give our lives entirely to him and learn from him, we will find that Jesus is gentle and humble in heart, not a brutal taskmaster who constantly pushes us to give more. In the span of three verses, Jesus twice promises rest for those who come to him. The conclusion of this brief passage is beautiful and hopeful:

> "Come to me, all you who are weary and burdened, and I will give you rest. Take my yoke upon you and learn from me, for I am gentle and humble in heart, and you will find rest for your souls. For my yoke is easy and my burden is light." (Matt. 11:28–30)

I want to conclude by inviting you to receive Jesus' easy yoke. This is something of a paradox. The easy yoke is receiving the gift of full salvation.

To the world, this seems impossible. Surely full salvation is a heavy yoke, and not where we find rest and relief from our heavy burdens?

We only experience the fullness of the love, joy, and peace that God intends for us when we receive power from God to walk in freedom, in purity, and in harmony with God's will.

The easy way of the world turns out to be the hardest of all. This way leads to relational damage, stress and sleepless nights, guilt and shame, anger and hatred, hopelessness and despair, and a lack of peace and connection with God, yourself, and others.

The cultural stereotype of growth in holiness being an unwelcome and impossible burden is a distortion of the real thing. The witness of those who have gone before us is not one of exhaustion from constant striving and disappointment in always falling short. Those who have gone before us, who have received this grand depositum, testify to joy and intimacy with the Lord and a soul that is at rest because it abides in the perfect love of God given to us in Christ Jesus.

Come, Holy Spirit. Do it again!

Appendix A

The Nature, Design, and General Rules of Our United Societies[1]

In the latter end of the year 1739 eight or ten persons came to Mr. Wesley, in London, who appeared to be deeply convinced of sin, and earnestly groaning for redemption. They desired, as did two or three more the next day, that he would spend some time with them in prayer, and advise them how to flee from the wrath to come, which they saw continually hanging over their heads. That he might have more time for this great work, he appointed a day when they might all come together, which from thenceforward they did every week, namely, on Thursday in the evening. To these, and as many more as desired to join with them (for their number increased daily), he gave those advices from time to time which he judged most needful for them, and they always concluded their meeting with prayer suited to their several necessities.

This was the rise of the **United Society,** first in Europe, and then in America. Such a society is no other than "a company of men having the *form* and seeking the *power* of godliness, united in order to pray together, to receive the word of exhortation, and to watch over one another in love, that they may help each other to work out their salvation."

That it may the more easily be discerned whether they are indeed working out their own salvation, each society is divided into smaller companies, called **classes,** according to their respective places of abode. There are about twelve persons in a class, one of whom is styled the **leader.** It is his duty:

1. To see each person in his class once a week at least, in order: (1) to inquire how their souls prosper; (2) to advise, reprove, comfort or exhort, as occasion may require; (3) to receive what they are willing to give toward the relief of the preachers, church, and poor.
2. To meet the ministers and the stewards of the society once a week, in order: (1) to inform the minister of any that are sick, or of any that walk disorderly and will not be reproved; (2) to pay the stewards what they have received of their several classes in the week preceding.

There is only one condition previously required of those who desire admission into these societies: "a desire to flee from the wrath to come, and to be saved from their sins." But wherever this is really fixed in the soul it will be shown by its fruits.

It is therefore expected of all who continue therein that they should continue to evidence their desire of salvation,

First: By doing no harm, by avoiding evil of every kind, especially that which is most generally practiced, such as:

The taking of the name of God in vain.

The profaning the day of the Lord, either by doing ordinary work therein or by buying or selling.

Drunkenness: buying or selling spirituous liquors, or drinking them, unless in cases of extreme necessity.

Slaveholding; buying or selling slaves.

Fighting, quarreling, brawling, brother going to law with brother; returning evil for evil, or railing for railing; the using many words in buying or selling.

The buying or selling goods that have not paid the duty.

The giving or taking things on usury—i.e., unlawful interest.

Uncharitable or unprofitable conversation; particularly speaking evil of magistrates or of ministers.

Doing to others as we would not they should do unto us.

Doing what we know is not for the glory of God, as:

The putting on of gold and costly apparel.

The taking such diversions as cannot be used in the name of the Lord Jesus.

The singing those songs, or reading those books, which do not tend to the knowledge or love of God.

Softness and needless self-indulgence.

Laying up treasure upon earth.

Borrowing without a probability of paying; or taking up goods without a probability of paying for them.

It is expected of all who continue in these societies that they should continue to evidence their desire of salvation,

Secondly: By doing good; by being in every kind merciful after their power; as they have opportunity, doing good of every possible sort, and, as far as possible, to all men:

To their bodies, of the ability which God giveth, by giving food to the hungry, by clothing the naked, by visiting or helping them that are sick or in prison.

To their souls, by instructing, reproving, or exhorting all we have any intercourse with; trampling under foot that enthusiastic doctrine that "we are not to do good unless *our hearts be free to it.*"

By doing good, especially to them that are of the household of faith or groaning so to be; employing them preferably to others; buying one of another, helping each other in business, and so much the more because the world will love its own and them only.

By all possible diligence and frugality, that the gospel be not blamed.

By running with patience the race which is set before them, denying themselves, and taking up their cross daily; submitting to bear the reproach of Christ, to be as the filth and offscouring of the world; and looking that men should say all manner of evil of them *falsely*, for the Lord's sake.

It is expected of all who desire to continue in these societies that they should continue to evidence their desire of salvation,

Thirdly: By attending upon all the ordinances of God; such are:

The public worship of God.

The ministry of the Word, either read or expounded.

The Supper of the Lord.

Family and private prayer.

Searching the Scriptures.

Fasting or abstinence.

These are the General Rules of our societies; all of which we are taught of God to observe, even in his written Word, which is the only rule, and the sufficient rule, both of our faith and practice. And all these we know his Spirit writes on truly awakened hearts. If there be any among us who observe them not, who habitually break any of them, let it be known unto them who watch over that soul as they who must give an account. We will admonish him of the error of his ways. We will bear with him for a season. But then, if he repent not, he hath no more place among us. We have delivered our own souls.

Appendix B

Rules of the Band Societies[1]

Rules of the Band Societies Drawn up Dec. 25, 1738

The design of our meeting is to obey that command of God, "Confess your faults one to another, and pray one for another that ye may be healed."

To this end we intend:

1. To meet once a week, at the least.
2. To come punctually at the hour appointed, without some extraordinary reason.
3. To begin (those of us who are present) exactly at the hour, with singing or prayer.
4. To speak, each of us in order, freely and plainly the true state of our souls, with the faults we have committed in thought, word, or deed, and the temptations we have felt since our last meeting.

5. To end every meeting with prayer, suited to the state of each person present.
6. To desire some person among us to speak *his* own state first, and then to ask the rest in order as many and as searching questions as may be concerning their state, sins, and temptations.

Some of the questions proposed to every one before *he* is admitted amongst us may be to this effect:

1. Have you the forgiveness of your sins?
2. Have you peace with God, through our Lord Jesus Christ?
3. Have you the witness of God's Spirit with your spirit that you are a child of God?
4. Is the love of God shed abroad in your heart?
5. Has no sin, inward or outward, dominion over you?
6. Do you desire to be told of your faults?
7. Do you desire to be told of all your faults, and that plain and home?
8. Do you desire that every one of us should tell you from time to time whatsoever is in *his* heart concerning you?
9. Consider! Do you desire we should tell you whatsoever we think, whatsoever we fear, whatsoever we hear, concerning you?
10. Do you desire that in doing this we should come as close as possible, that we should cut to the quick, and search your heart to the bottom?
11. Is it your desire and design to be on this and all other occasions entirely open, so as to speak everything that is in your heart, without exception, without disguise, and without reserve?

Any of the preceding questions may be asked as often as occasion offers; the five following at every meeting:

1. What known sins have you committed since our last meeting?
2. What temptations have you met with?
3. How were you delivered?
4. What have you thought, said, or done, of which you doubt whether it be sin or not?
5. Have you nothing you desire to keep secret?

Appendix C

John Wesley's Sermon on Christian Perfection[1]

"Not as though I had already attained,
either were already perfect."

—Phil. 3:12 KJV

Should Perfection Be Sought After?

1. There is scarce any expression in Holy Writ which has given more offense than this. The word *perfect* is what many cannot bear. The very sound of it is an abomination to them. And whosoever preaches perfection (as the phrase is) that is, asserts that it is attainable in this life, runs great hazard of being accounted by them worse than a heathen man or a publican.

2. And hence some have advised wholly to lay aside the use of those expressions "because they have given so great offense." But

are they not found in the oracles of God? If so, by what authority can any messenger of God lay them aside, even though all men should be offended? We have not so learned Christ; neither may we thus give place to the devil. Whatsoever God has spoken that will we speak, whether men will hear or whether they will forbear; knowing that then alone can any minister of Christ be "pure from the blood of all men," when he has "not shunned to declare unto them all the counsel of God" [Acts 20:26–27].

3. We may not, therefore, lay these expressions aside, seeing they are the words of God, and not of man. But we may and ought to explain the meaning of them, that those who are sincere of heart may not err to the right hand or to the left, from the mark of the prize of their high calling. And this is the more needful to be done because in the verse already repeated the apostle speaks of himself as not perfect: "Not," says he, "as though I were already perfect." And yet immediately after, in the fifteenth verse, he speaks of himself, yea and many others, as perfect. "Let us," says he, "as many as be perfect, be thus minded" [Phil. 3:15].

4. In order, therefore, to remove the difficulty arising from this seeming contradiction, as well as to give light to them who are pressing forward to the mark, and that those who are lame be not turned out of the way, I shall endeavor to show, first, in what sense Christians are not; and, secondly, in what sense they are, perfect.

I. What Is *Not* Meant by Christian Perfection

Ignorance

1. In the first place I shall endeavor to show in what sense Christians are not perfect. And both from experience and

Scripture it appears, first, that they are not perfect in knowledge: they are not so perfect in this life as to be free from ignorance. They know, it may be, in common with other men, many things relating to the present world; and they know, with regard to the world to come, the general truths which God has revealed. They know, likewise, (what the natural man receives not, for these things are spiritually discerned) "what manner of love" it is wherewith "the Father" has loved them, "that they should be called the sons of God" [1 John 3:1]. They know the mighty working of his Spirit in their hearts [Eph. 3:16]; and the wisdom of his providence, directing all their paths [Prov. 3:6] and causing all things to work together for their good [Rom. 8:28]. Yea, they know in every circumstance of life what the Lord requires of them, and how to keep a conscience void of offence both toward God and toward man [Acts 24:16].

2. But innumerable are the things which they know not. Touching the Almighty himself, they cannot search him out to perfection. "Lo, these are but a part of his ways; but the thunder of his power who can understand" [Job 26:14]. They cannot understand, I will not say, how "there are three that bear record in heaven, the Father, the Son, and the Holy Spirit, and these three are one" [1 John 5:7]; or how the eternal Son of God "took upon himself the form of a servant" [Phil. 2:7];—but not any one attribute, not any one circumstance of the divine nature [2 Peter 1:4]. Neither is it for them to know the times and seasons [Acts 1:7] when God will work his great works upon the earth; no, not even those which he has in part revealed by his servants and prophets since the world began [see Amos 3:7]. Much less do they know when God, having "accomplished the number of his elect, will hasten his kingdom"; when "the heavens shall pass

away with a great noise, and the elements shall melt with fervent heat" [2 Peter 3:10].

3. They know not the reasons even of many of his present dispensations with the sons of men; but are constrained to rest here,—Though "clouds and darkness are round about him, righteousness and judgment are the habitation of his seat" [Ps. 97:2]. Yes, often with regard to his dealings with themselves, does their Lord say unto them, "What I do, you know not now; but you shall know hereafter" [John 13:7]. And how little do they know of what is ever before them, of even the visible works of his hands! How "he spreads the north over the empty place, and hangs the earth upon nothing" [Job 26:7]. How he unites all the parts of this vast machine by a secret chain which cannot be broken. So great is the ignorance, so very little the knowledge, of even the best of men!

Mistakes

4. No one, then, is so perfect in this life, as to be free from ignorance. Nor, secondly, from mistake; which indeed is almost an unavoidable consequence of it; seeing those who "know but in part" [1 Cor. 13:12] are ever liable to err touching the things which they know not. It is true, the children of God do not mistake as to the things essential to salvation: They do not "put darkness for light, or light for darkness" [Isa. 5:20]; neither "seek death in the error of their life" [Wisdom 1:12]. For they are "taught of God," and the way which he teaches them, the way of holiness, is so plain, that "the wayfaring man, though a fool, need not err therein" [Isa. 35:8]. But in things unessential to salvation they do err, and that frequently.

The best and wisest of men are frequently mistaken even with regard to facts; believing those things not to have been which really were, or those to have been done which were not. Or, suppose they are not mistaken as to the fact itself, they may be with regard to its circumstances; believing them, or many of them, to have been quite different from what in truth, they were. And hence cannot but arise many farther mistakes. Hence they may believe either past or present actions which were or are evil, to be good; and such as were or are good, to be evil. Hence also they may judge not according to truth with regard to the characters of men; and that, not only by supposing good men to be better, or wicked men to be worse, than they are, but by believing them to have been or to be good men who were or are very wicked; or perhaps those to have been or to be wicked men, who were or are holy and unreprovable.

5. No, with regard to the Holy Scriptures themselves, as careful as they are to avoid it, the best of men are liable to mistake, and do mistake day by day; especially with respect to those parts thereof which less immediately relate to practice. Hence even the children of God are not agreed as to the interpretation of many places in Holy Writ. Nor is their difference of opinion any proof that they are not the children of God on either side; but it is a proof that we are no more to expect any living man to be infallible than to be omniscient.

6. If it be objected to what has been observed under this and the preceding head, that St. John, speaking to his brethren in the faith says, "You have an unction from the Holy One, and you know all things" (1 John 2:20). The answer is plain: "You know all things that are needful for your souls' health" [cf. 3 John 2]. That the apostle never designed to extend this farther, that

he could not speak it in an absolute sense, is clear. First from hence, that otherwise he would describe the disciple as "above his Master"; seeing Christ himself, as man, knew not all things: "Of that hour," says he, "knows no man; no, not the Son, but the Father only" [Mark 13:32]. It is clear, secondly, from the apostle's own words that follow: "These things have I written unto you concerning them that deceive you" [cf. 1 John 3:7]; as well as from his frequently repeated caution, "Let no man deceive you" [see Mark 13:5; Eph. 5:6; 2 Thess. 2:3], which had been altogether needless, had not those very persons who had that unction from the Holy One [1 John 2:20] been liable, not to ignorance only, but to mistake also.

Infirmities

7. Even Christians, therefore, are not so perfect as to be free either from ignorance or error. We may, thirdly, add, nor from infirmities. Only let us take care to understand this word aright; only let us not give that soft title to known sins, as the manner of some is. So, one man tells us, "Every man has his infirmity, and mine is drunkenness"; another has the infirmity of uncleanness; another of taking God's holy name in vain; and yet another has the infirmity of calling his brother, "You fool" [Matt. 5:22], or returning "railing for railing" [1 Peter 3:9]. It is plain that all you who speak, if you repent not, shall, with your infirmities, go quick into hell! But I mean hereby, not only those which are properly termed bodily infirmities, but all those inward or outward imperfections which are not of a moral nature. Such are the weakness or slowness of understanding, dullness or confusedness of apprehension, incoherency of thought, irregular quickness or

heaviness of imagination. Such (to mention no more of this kind) is the want of a ready or of a retentive memory.

Such in another kind, are those which are commonly, in some measure, consequent upon these; namely, slowness of speech, impropriety of language, ungracefulness of pronunciation; to which one might add a thousand nameless defects, either in conversation or behavior. These are the infirmities which are found in the best of men, in a larger or smaller proportion. And from these none can hope to be perfectly freed till the spirit returns to God that gave it [Eccles. 12:7].

Temptation

8. Nor can we expect, till then, to be wholly free from temptation. Such perfection belongs not to this life. It is true, there are those who, being given up to work all uncleanness with greediness [Eph. 4:19], scarce perceive the temptations which they resist not, and so seem to be without temptation. There are also many whom the wise enemy of souls, seeing to be fast asleep in the dead form of godliness, will not tempt to gross sin, lest they should awake before they drop into everlasting burnings. I know there are also children of God who, being now justified freely [Rom. 5:1], having found redemption in the blood of Christ [Eph. 1:7], for the present feel no temptation. God has said to their enemies, "Touch not mine anointed, and do my children no harm" [see 1 Chron. 16:22]. And for this season, it may be for weeks or months, he causes them to "ride on high places" [Deut. 32:13]; he bears them as on eagles' wings [Ex. 19:4], above all the fiery darts of the wicked one [Eph. 6:16]. But this state will not last always; as we may learn from that single consideration,

that the Son of God himself, in the days of his flesh, was tempted even to the end of his life [Heb. 2:18; 4:15; 6:7]. Therefore, so let his servant expect to be; for "it is enough that he be as his Master" [Luke 6:40].

9. Christian perfection, therefore, does not imply (as some men seem to have imagined) an exemption either from ignorance or mistake, or infirmities or temptations. Indeed, it is only another term for holiness. They are two names for the same thing. Thus everyone that is perfect is holy, and everyone that is holy is, in the Scripture sense, perfect. Yet we may, lastly, observe, that neither in this respect is there any absolute perfection on earth. There is no perfection of degrees, as it is termed; none which does not admit of a continual increase. So that how much so ever any man has attained, or in how high a degree so ever he is perfect, he has still need to "grow in grace" [2 Peter 3:18], and daily to advance in the knowledge and love of God his Savior [see Phil. 1:9].

II. What *Is* Meant by Christian Perfection

Babes in Christ

1. In what sense, then, are Christians perfect? This is what I shall endeavor, in the second place, to show. But it should be premised, that there are several stages in Christian life, as in natural; some of the children of God being but newborn babes; others having attained to more maturity. And accordingly St. John, in his first Epistle (1 John 2:12, &c.) applies himself severally to those he terms little children, those he styles young men, and those whom he entitles fathers. "I write unto you, little children," says the apostle, "because your sins are forgiven you." Because thus far

you have attained, being "justified freely," you "have peace with God, through Jesus Christ" [Rom. 5:1]. "I write unto you, young men, because you have overcome the wicked one"; or (as he afterward adds) "because you are strong, and the word of God abides in you" [1 John 2:13–14]. You have quenched the fiery darts of the wicked one [Eph. 6:16], the doubts and fears wherewith he disturbed your first peace; and the witness of God, that your sins are forgiven, now abides in your heart. "I write unto you, fathers, because ye have known him that is from the beginning" [1 John 2:13]. You have known both the Father and the Son and the Spirit of Christ, in your inmost soul. You are "perfect men, being grown up to the measure of the stature of the fullness of Christ" [Eph. 4:13].

2. It is of these chiefly I speak in the latter part of this discourse, for these only are properly Christians. But even babes in Christ are in such a sense perfect, or born of God (an expression taken also in diverse senses) as, first, not to commit sin. If any doubt of this privilege of the sons of God, the question is not to be decided by abstract reasonings, which may be drawn out into an endless length, and leave the point just as it was before. Neither is it to be determined by the experience of this or that particular person. Many may suppose they do not commit sin, when they do; but this proves nothing either way. To the law and to the testimony we appeal, "Let God be true, and every man a liar" [Rom. 3:4]. By his Word will we abide, and that alone. Hereby we ought to be judged.

3. Now the Word of God plainly declares, that even those who are justified, who are born again in the lowest sense, "do not continue in sin"; that they cannot "live any longer therein" (Rom. 6:1–2); that they are "planted together in the likeness of

the death" of Christ (Rom. 6:5); that their "old man is crucified with him," the body of sin being destroyed, so that henceforth they do not serve sin; that being dead with Christ, they are free from sin (Rom. 6:6–7); that they are "dead unto sin, and alive unto God" (Rom. 6:11); that "sin has no more dominion over them," who are "not under the law, but under grace"; but that these, "being free from sin, are become the servants of righteousness" (Rom. 6:14, 18).

Freedom from Outward Sin

4. The very least which can be implied in these words, is that the persons spoken of therein, namely, all real Christians, or believers in Christ, are made free from outward sin. And the same freedom, which St. Paul here expresses in such variety of phrases, St. Peter expresses in that one: (1 Peter 4:1–2): "He that has suffered in the flesh has ceased from sin, that he no longer should live to the desires of men, but to the will of God." For this ceasing from sin, if it be interpreted in the lowest sense, as regarding only the outward behavior, must denote the ceasing from the outward act, from any outward transgression of the law.

5. But most express are the well-known words of St. John, in the third chapter of his First Epistle, verse 8, &c.: "He that commits sin is of the devil; for the devil sins from the beginning. For this purpose the Son of God was manifested, that he might destroy the works of the devil. Whosoever is born of God does not commit sin; for his seed remains in him: And he cannot sin because he is born of God" [1 John 3:8–9]. And those in the fifth: "We know that whosoever is born of God sins not; but he that is begotten of God keeps himself, and that wicked one touches him not" (1 John 5:18).

6. Indeed it is said this means only, he sins not willfully; or he does not commit sin habitually; or, not as other men do; or, not as he did before. But by whom is this said? By St. John? No. There is no such word in the text; nor in the whole chapter; nor in all his Epistle; nor in any part of his writings whatsoever. Why then, the best way to answer a bold assertion is simply to deny it. And if any man can prove it from the Word of God, let him bring forth his strong reasons.

Freedom from Habitual Sin

7. And a sort of reason there is, which has been frequently brought to support these strange assertions, drawn from the examples recorded in the Word of God: "What!" say they, "did not Abraham himself commit sin—prevaricating, and denying his wife? Did not Moses commit sin, when he provoked God at the waters of strife? No, to produce one for all, did not even David, 'the man after God's own heart,' commit sin, in the matter of Uriah the Hittite; even murder and adultery?" It is most sure he did. All this is true. But what is it you would infer from hence? It may be granted, first, that David, in the general course of his life, was one of the holiest men among the Jews; and, secondly, that the holiest men among the Jews did sometimes commit sin. But if you would hence infer, that all Christians do and must commit sin as long as they live; this consequence we utterly deny: It will never follow from those premises.

8. Those who argue thus seem never to have considered that declaration of our Lord: (Matt. 11:11): "Verily I say unto you, Among them that are born of women there hath not risen a greater than John the Baptist: Notwithstanding he that is least in the kingdom of heaven is greater than he." I fear, indeed, there are

some who have imagined "the kingdom of heaven," here, to mean the kingdom of glory; as if the Son of God had just discovered to us, that the least glorified saint in heaven is greater than any man upon earth! To mention this is sufficiently to refute it. There can, therefore, no doubt be made, but "the kingdom of heaven" here (as in the following verse, where it is said to be taken by force) [Matt. 11:12] or, "the kingdom of God," as St. Luke expresses it, is that kingdom of God on earth whereunto all true believers in Christ, all real Christians, belong. In these words, then, our Lord declares two things: first, that before his coming in the flesh, among all the children of men there had not been one greater than John the Baptist; whence it evidently follows, that neither Abraham, David, nor any Jew was greater than John.

Our Lord, secondly, declares that he which is least in the kingdom of God (in that kingdom which he came to set up on earth, and which the violent now began to take by force) is greater than he; not a greater prophet as some have interpreted the word; for this is palpably false in fact; but greater in the grace of God, and the knowledge of our Lord Jesus Christ. Therefore, we cannot measure the privileges of real Christians by those formerly given to the Jews. Their "ministration" (or dispensation) we allow "was glorious"; but ours "exceeds in glory" [2 Cor. 3:7–9]. So that whosoever would bring down the Christian dispensation to the Jewish standard, whosoever gleans up the examples of weakness, recorded in the Law and the Prophets, and thence infers that they who have "put on Christ" [Gal. 3:27] are endued with no greater strength, does greatly err, neither "knowing the Scriptures, nor the power of God" [Matt. 22:29].

9. "But are there not assertions in Scripture which prove the same thing, if it cannot be inferred from those examples? Does

not the Scripture say expressly, 'Even a just man sins seven times a day?'" I answer no. The Scripture says no such thing. There is no such text in all the Bible. That which seems to be intended is the sixteenth verse of the twenty-fourth chapter of the Proverbs the words of which are these: "A just man falls seven times, and rises up again" [Prov. 24:16]. But this is quite another thing. For, first, the words "a day" are not in the text. So that if a just man falls seven times in his life, it is as much as is affirmed here. Secondly, here is no mention of falling into sin at all; what is here mentioned is falling into temporal affliction. This plainly appears from the verse before, the words of which are these: "Lay not wait, O wicked man, against the dwelling of the righteous; spoil not his resting place" [Prov. 24:15]. It follows, "For a just man falls seven times, and rises up again; but the wicked shall fall into mischief." As if he had said, "God will deliver him out of his trouble; but when you fall, there shall be none to deliver you."

Justified through Christ

10. "But, however, in other places," continue the objectors, "Solomon does assert plainly, 'There is no man that sins not' (1 Kings 8:46; 2 Chron. 6:36); yes, 'There is not a just man upon earth that does good, and sins not' (Eccles. 7:20)." I answer, without doubt, thus it was in the days of Solomon. Yes, thus it was from Adam to Moses, from Moses to Solomon, and from Solomon to Christ. There was then no man that sinned not. Even from the day that sin entered into the world, there was not a just man upon earth that did good and sinned not, until the Son of God was manifested to take away our sins. It is unquestionably true, that "the heir, as long as he is a child, differs nothing from

a servant" [Gal. 4:1]. And that even so they (all the holy men of old, who were under the Jewish dispensation) were, during that infant state of the church, "in bondage under the elements of the world" [Gal. 4:3]. "But when the fullness of the time was come, God sent forth his Son, made under the law, to redeem them that were under the law, that they might receive the adoption of sons" [Gal. 4:4]; that they might receive that "grace which is now made manifest by the appearing of our Savior, Jesus Christ, who hath abolished death, and brought life and immortality to light through the gospel" (2 Tim. 1:10). Now, therefore, they "are no more servants, but sons" [see Gal. 4:7]. So that, whatsoever was the case of those under the law, we may safely affirm with St. John, that, since the gospel was given, "he that is born of God sins not" [1 John 5:18].

11. It is of great importance to observe, and that more carefully than is commonly done, the wide difference there is between the Jewish and the Christian dispensation; and that ground of it which the same apostle assigns in the seventh chapter of his Gospel (John 7:38, &c). After he had there related, those words of our blessed Lord, "He that believes me, as the Scripture has said, out of his belly shall flow rivers of living water," he immediately subjoins, "This spoke he of the Spirit," *ού ἔμελλον λαμβάνειν οἱ πιτεύοντες εἰς αὐτόν* [The believers will receive them in the future]—which they who should believe on him were afterward to receive. For the Holy Spirit was not yet given, because that Jesus was not yet glorified" [John 7:39].

Now, the apostle cannot mean here (as some have taught) that the miracle-working power of the Holy Spirit was not yet given. For this was given; our Lord had given it to all the apostles, when he first sent them forth to preach the gospel. He then gave them power over unclean spirits to cast them out; power to heal the sick; yes, to raise the dead [Mark 10:8]. But the Holy Spirit was not yet given in his sanctifying graces, as he was after Jesus was glorified. It was then when "he ascended up on high, and led captivity captive," that he "received" those "gifts for men, yea, even for the rebellious, that the Lord God might dwell among them" [Ps. 68:18; cf. Eph. 4:8]. And when the day of Pentecost was fully come [Acts 2:1] then first it was, that they who "waited for the promise of the Father" [Acts 1:4] were made more than conquerors [Rom. 8:37] over sin by the Holy Spirit given unto them.

12. That this great salvation from sin was not given till Jesus was glorified, St. Peter also plainly testifies; where, speaking of his brethren in the flesh, as now "receiving the end of their faith, the salvation of their souls," he adds (1 Peter 1:9, 10, &c) "Of which salvation the Prophets have inquired and searched diligently, who prophesied of the grace" that is, the gracious dispensation, "that should come unto you: Searching what, or what manner of time the Spirit of Christ which was in them did signify, when it testified beforehand the sufferings of Christ and the glory," the glorious salvation, "that should follow. Unto whom it was revealed, that not unto themselves, but unto us they did minister the things which are now reported unto you by them that have preached the gospel unto you with the Holy Ghost sent down from heaven" [1 Peter 1:12]; viz., at the day of Pentecost, and so unto all generations, into the hearts of all true believers. On this ground, even "the grace which was brought unto them by the revelation of Jesus Christ" [1 Peter 1:13], the apostle might well build that strong exhortation, "Wherefore girding up the loins of your mind, as he which hath called you is holy, so be ye holy in all manner of conversation" [1 Peter 1:13].

13. Those who have duly considered these things must allow that the privileges of Christians are in no way to be measured

by what the Old Testament records concerning those who were under the Jewish dispensation; seeing the fullness of times is now come; the Holy Spirit is now given; the great salvation of God is brought unto men by the revelation of Jesus Christ. The kingdom of heaven is now set up on earth; concerning which the Spirit of God declared of old (so far is David from being the pattern or standard of Christian perfection), "He that is feeble among them at that day, shall be as David; and the house of David shall be as God, as the angel of the Lord before them" (Zech. 12:8).

God's Grace Provides a Way to Avoid Temptation

14. If, therefore, you would prove that the apostle's words, "He that is born of God sins not," [1 John 5:18] are not to be understood according to their plain, natural, obvious meaning, it is from the New Testament you are to bring your proofs, else you will fight as one that beats the air [1 Cor. 9:26]. And the first of these which is usually brought is taken from the examples recorded in the New Testament. "The apostles themselves," it is said, "committed sin; nay, the greatest of them, Peter and Paul: St. Paul, by his sharp contention with Barnabas [Acts 15:39]; and St. Peter, by his dissimulation at Antioch" [Gal. 2:11]. Well, suppose both Peter and Paul did then commit sin; what is it you would infer from hence? That all the other apostles committed sin sometimes? There is no shadow of proof in this. Or would you thence infer, that all the other Christians of the apostolic age committed sin? Worse and worse: this is such an inference as, one would imagine, a man in his senses could never have thought of. Or will you argue thus, "If two of the apostles did once commit sin, then all other Christians, in all ages, do and will commit sin as long as they live"?

Alas, my brother, a child of common understanding would be ashamed of such reasoning as this! Least of all can you with any color of argument infer, that any man must commit sin at all. No, God forbid we should thus speak! No necessity of sinning was laid upon them. The grace of God was surely sufficient for them. And it is sufficient for us at this day. With the temptation which fell on them, there was a way to escape; as there is to every soul of man in every temptation. So that whosoever is tempted to any sin, need not yield; for no man is tempted above that he is able to bear [1 Cor. 10:13].

Strength Made Perfect in Weakness

15. "But St. Paul besought the Lord thrice, and yet he could not escape from his temptation." Let us consider his own words literally translated: "There was given to me a thorn to the flesh, an angel (or messenger) of Satan, to buffet me. Touching this, I besought the Lord thrice, that it (or he) might depart from me. And he said unto me, My grace is sufficient for you: For my strength is made perfect in weakness. Most gladly, therefore, will I rather glory in" these "my weaknesses, that the strength of Christ may rest upon me. Therefore I take pleasure in weaknesses; for when I am weak, then am I strong" [2 Cor. 12:7–10].

16. As this scripture is one of the strongholds of the patrons of sin, it may be proper to weigh it thoroughly. Let it be observed then, first, it does by no means appear that this thorn, whatsoever it was, occasioned St. Paul to commit sin; much less laid him under any necessity of doing so. Therefore, from hence it can never be proved that any Christian must commit sin. Secondly, the ancient Fathers inform us, it was bodily pain: "a violent headache," says Tertullian; (De Pudic.); to which both Chrysostom

and St. Jerome agree. St. Cyprian [De Mortalitate] expresses it, a little more generally, in those terms: "Many and grievous torments of the flesh and of the body." Thirdly, to this exactly agree the apostle's own words, "A thorn to the flesh to smite, beat, or buffet me." "My strength is made perfect in weakness," which same word occurs no less than four times in these two verses only. But, fourthly, whatsoever it was, it could not be either inward or outward sin. It could no more be inward stirrings, than outward expressions, of pride, anger, or lust. This is manifest, beyond all possible exception from the words that immediately follow, "Most gladly will I glory in" these "my weaknesses, that the strength of Christ may rest upon me" [2 Cor. 12:9]. What! Did he glory in pride, in anger, in lust? Was it through these weaknesses, that the strength of Christ rested upon him, he goes on, "Therefore I take pleasure in weaknesses; for when I am weak, then am I strong" [2 Cor. 12:10]; that is, when I am weak in body, then am I strong in spirit. But will any man dare to say, "When I am weak by pride or lust, then am I strong in spirit" I call you all to record this day, who find the strength of Christ resting upon you, can you glory in anger, or pride, or lust? Can you take pleasure in these infirmities? Do these weaknesses make you strong? Would you not leap into hell, were it possible, to escape them? Even by yourselves, then judge whether the apostle could glory and take pleasure in them!

Let it be, lastly, observed, that this thorn was given to St. Paul above fourteen years before he wrote this Epistle [2 Cor. 12:2]; which itself was wrote several years before he finished his course [see Acts 20:24; 2 Tim. 4:7]. So that he had after this, a long course to run, many battles to fight, many victories to gain, and great increase to receive in all the gifts of God, and the knowledge of Jesus Christ. Therefore from any spiritual weakness (if such it had been) which he at that time felt, we could by no means infer that he was never made strong; that Paul the aged, the father in Christ, still labored under the same weaknesses; that he was in no higher state till the day of his death. From all which it appears that this instance of St. Paul is quite foreign to the question, and does in no wise clash with the assertion of St. John, "He that is born of God sins not" [1 John 5:18].

Justified by Christ's Forgiveness

17. "But does not St. James directly contradict this his words are, 'In many things we offend all' (James 3:2) and is not offending the same as committing sin"? In this place, I allow it is: I allow the persons here spoken of did commit sin; yes, that they all committed many sins. But who are the persons here spoken of? Why, those many masters or teachers whom God had not sent (probably the same vain men who taught that faith without works, which is so sharply reproved in the preceding chapter) (James 2); not the apostle himself, nor any real Christian. That in the word we (used by a figure of speech common in all other, as well as the inspired, writings) the apostle could not possibly include himself or any other true believer, appears evidently, first, from the same word in the ninth verse: "Therewith," says he, "bless we God and therewith curse we men. Out of the same mouth proceeds blessing and cursing" [James 3:9]. True, but not out of the mouth of the apostle, nor of anyone who is in Christ a new creature [2 Cor. 5:17].

Secondly, from the verse immediately preceding the text, and manifestly connected with it: "My brethren, be not many masters" (or teachers) "knowing that we shall receive the greater condemnation." "For in many things we offend all" [James 3:2]. We! Who not the apostles, not true believers; but they who know they should receive the greater condemnation, because of those many offenses. But this could not be spoke of the apostle himself, or of any who trod in his steps, seeing "there is no condemnation to them who walk not after the flesh, but after the Spirit" [Rom. 8:1].

No, thirdly, the very verse itself proves, that "we offend all," cannot be spoken either of all men, or of all Christians; for in it there immediately follows the mention of a man who offends not, as the we first mentioned did; from whom, therefore, he is professedly contradistinguished, and pronounced a perfect man.

18. So clearly does St. James explain himself, and fix the meaning of his own words. Yet, lest anyone should still remain in doubt, St. John, writing many years after St. James, puts the matter entirely out of dispute, by the express declarations above recited. But here a fresh difficulty may arise: How shall we reconcile St. John with himself? In one place he declares, "Whosoever is born of God does not commit sin" [1 John 3:9]; and again, "We know that he which is born of God sins not" [1 John 5:18]. And yet in another he says, "If we say that we have no sin, we deceive ourselves, and the truth is not in us" [1 John 1:8]; and again, "If we say that we have not sinned, we make him a liar, and his word is not in us" [1 John 1:10].

19. As great a difficulty as this may at first appear, it vanishes away, if we observe, first, that the tenth verse fixes the sense of the eighth: "If we say we have no sin," in the former, being explained by, "If we say we have not sinned," in the latter verse [1 John 1:10, 8]. Secondly, that the point under present

consideration is not whether we have or have not sinned heretofore; and neither of these verses asserts that we do sin, or commit sin now. Thirdly, that the ninth verse explains both the eighth and tenth. "If we confess our sins, he is faithful and just to forgive us our sins, and to cleanse us from all unrighteousness." As if he had said, "I have before affirmed, 'The blood of Jesus Christ cleanses us from all sin; but let no man say, I need it not; I have no sin to be cleansed from. If we say that we have no sin, that we have not sinned, we deceive ourselves, and make God a liar: But if we confess our sins, he is faithful and just,' not only 'to forgive our sins,' but also 'to cleanse us from all unrighteousness:' [1 John 1:8–10] that we may 'go and sin no more'" [John 8:11].

20. St. John, therefore, is well consistent with himself, as well as with the other holy writers; as will yet more evidently appear if we place all his assertions touching this matter in one view: he declares, first, the blood of Jesus Christ cleanses us from all sin. Secondly, no man can say, I have not sinned, I have no sin to be cleansed from. Thirdly, but God is ready both to forgive our past sins and to save us from them for the time to come [1 John 1:7–10]. Fourthly, "These things I write unto you," says the apostle, "that ye may not sin. But if any man" should "sin," or have sinned (as the word might be rendered) he need not continue in sin; seeing "we have an Advocate with the Father, Jesus Christ the righteous" [1 John 2:1–2]. Thus far all is clear. But lest any doubt should remain in a point of so vast importance, the apostle resumes this subject in the third chapter, and largely explains his own meaning. "Little children," says he, "let no man deceive you" (as though I had given any encouragement to those that continue in sin); "He that does righteousness is righteous, even as He is righteous. He that commits sin is of the devil; for the devil sins from

the beginning. For this purpose the Son of God was manifested, that he might destroy the works of the devil. Whosoever is born of God doth not commit sin: For his seed remains in him; and he cannot sin, because he is born of God. In this the children of God are manifest, and the children of the devil" (1 John 3:7–10). Here the point, which till then might possibly have admitted of some doubt in weak minds, is purposely settled by the last of the inspired writers, and decided in the clearest manner. In conformity, therefore, both to the doctrine of St. John, and to the whole tenor of the New Testament, we fix this conclusion—a Christian is so far perfect, as not to commit sin.

Freedom from Evil Thoughts and Tempers

21. This is the glorious privilege of every Christian; yes, though he be but a babe in Christ. But it is only of those who are strong in the Lord, and "have overcome the wicked one," or rather of those who "have known him that is from the beginning" [1 John 2:13–14], that it can be affirmed they are in such a sense perfect, as, secondly, to be freed from evil thoughts and evil tempers. First, from evil or sinful thoughts. But here let it be observed, that thoughts concerning evil are not always evil thoughts; that a thought concerning sin, and a sinful thought, are widely different. A man, for instance, may think of a murder which another has committed; and yet this is no evil or sinful thought. So our blessed Lord himself doubtless thought of, or understood the thing spoken by the devil, when he said, "All these things will I give you, if you will fall down and worship me" [Matt. 4:9]. Yet had he no evil or sinful thought; nor indeed was capable of having any. And even hence it follows, that neither have real Christians: for "every one

that is perfect is as his Master" (Luke 6:40). Therefore, if he was free from evil or sinful thoughts, so are they likewise.

22. And, indeed, whence should evil thoughts proceed, in the servant who is as his Master "Out of the heart of man" (if at all) "proceed evil thoughts" (Mark 7:21). If, therefore, his heart be no longer evil, then evil thoughts can no longer proceed out of it. If the tree were corrupt, so would be the fruit: but the tree is good; the fruit, therefore is good also (Matt. 22:33); our Lord himself bearing witness, "Every good tree brings forth good fruit. A good tree cannot bring forth evil fruit," as "a corrupt tree cannot bring forth good fruit" (Matt 7:17–18).

23. The same happy privilege of real Christians, St. Paul asserts from his own experience. "The weapons of our warfare," says he, "are not carnal, but mighty through God to the pulling down of strongholds; casting down imaginations" (or reasonings rather, for so the word *logismous* signifies; all the reasonings of pride and unbelief against the declarations, promises, or gifts of God) "and every high thing that exalts itself against the knowledge of God, and bringing into captivity every thought to the obedience of Christ" (2 Cor. 10:4, &c).

24. And as Christians indeed are freed from evil thoughts, so are they, secondly, from evil tempers. This is evident from the above-mentioned declaration of our Lord himself: "The disciple is not above his Master; but every one that is perfect shall be as his Master" [Luke 6:40]. He had been delivering, just before, some of the most sublime doctrines of Christianity, and some of the most grievous to flesh and blood. "I say unto you, love your enemies, do good to them which hate you; and unto him that smite you on the one cheek, offer also the other" [Luke 6:29]. Now these he well knew the world would not receive; and, therefore,

immediately adds, "Can the blind lead the blind? Will they not both fall into the ditch?" [Luke 6:39]. As if he had said, "Do not confer with flesh and blood touching these things, with men void of spiritual discernment, the eyes of whose understanding God hath not opened, lest they and you perish together." In the next verse he removes the two grand objections with which these wise fools meet us at every turn: "These things are too grievous to be borne" or, "They are too high to be attained" [Matt. 23:4] saying, "The disciple is not above his Master; therefore, if I have suffered, be content to tread in my steps. And doubt ye not then, but I will fulfill my word: 'For every one that is perfect shall be as his Master'" [Luke 6:40]. But his Master was free from all sinful tempers. So, therefore, is his disciple, even every real Christian.

25. Every one of these can say, with St. Paul, "I am crucified with Christ: Nevertheless I live; yet not I, but Christ lives in me" [Gal. 2:20]—words that manifestly describe a deliverance from inward as well as from outward sin. This is expressed both negatively, I live not (my evil nature, the body of sin, is destroyed); and positively, Christ lives in me; and, therefore, all that is holy, and just, and good. Indeed, both these, Christ lives in me, and I live not, are inseparably connected; for "what communion hath light with darkness, or Christ with Belial" [2 Cor. 6:15].

26. He, therefore, who lives in true believers, has "purified their hearts by faith" [Acts 15:9]; insomuch that every one that has Christ in him the hope of glory [Col. 1:27], "purifies himself, even as he is pure" (1 John 3:3). He is purified from pride; for Christ was lowly of heart [Matt. 11:29]. He is pure from self-will or desire; for Christ desired only to do the will of his Father, and to finish his work [John 4:34; 5:30]. And he is pure from anger, in the common sense of the word; for Christ was meek and

gentle, patient and long-suffering. I say, in the common sense of the word; for all anger is not evil. We read of our Lord himself [Mark 3:5] that he once "looked round with anger." But with what kind of anger? The next word shows, *sullupoumenos*, being, at the same time "grieved for the hardness of their hearts" [Mark 3:6]. So then he was angry at the sin, and in the same moment grieved for the sinners; angry or displeased at the offense, but sorry for the offenders. With anger, yes, hatred, he looked upon the thing; with grief and love upon the persons. Go, you that are perfect, and do likewise. Be thus angry, and sin not [see Eph. 4:26]; feeling a displacency at every offence against God, but only love and tender compassion to the offender.

27. Thus does Jesus "save his people from their sins" [Matt. 1:21]. And not only from outward sins, but also from the sins of their hearts; from evil thoughts and from evil tempers. "True," say some, "we shall thus be saved from our sins; but not till death; not in this world." But how are we to reconcile this with the express words of St. John? "Herein is our love made perfect, that we may have boldness in the day of judgment. Because as he is, so are we in this world." The apostle here, beyond all contradiction, speaks of himself and other living Christians, of whom (as though he had foreseen this very evasion, and set himself to overturn it from the foundation) he flatly affirms, that not only at or after death but in this world they are as their Master (1 John 4:17).

Freedom from Sin in This *World*

28. Exactly agreeable to this are his words in the first chapter of this Epistle (1 John 1:5, &c), "God is light, and in him is no

darkness at all. If we walk in the light, we have fellowship one with another, and the blood of Jesus Christ his Son cleanses us from all sin." And again, "If we confess our sins, he is faithful and just to forgive us our sins, and to cleanse us from all unrighteousness" [1 John 1:9]. Now it is evident, the apostle here also speaks of a deliverance wrought in this world. For he says not, the blood of Christ will cleanse at the hour of death, or in the day of judgment, but, it "cleanses," at the time present, "us," living Christians, "from all sin." And it is equally evident, that if any sin remain, we are not cleansed from all sin. If any unrighteousness remain in the soul, it is not cleansed from all unrighteousness. Neither let any sinner against his own soul say that this relates to justification only or the cleansing us from the guilt of sin. First, because this is confounding together what the apostle clearly distinguishes, who mentions first, to forgive us our sins, and then to cleanse us from all unrighteousness. Secondly, because this is asserting justification by works, in the strongest sense possible; it is making all inward as well as outward holiness necessarily previous to justification. For if the cleansing here spoken of is no other than the cleansing us from the guilt of sin, then we are not cleansed from guilt; that is, are not justified, unless on condition of "walking in the light, as he is in the light" [1 John 1:7]. It remains, then, that Christians are saved in this world from all sin, from all unrighteousness; that they are now in such a sense perfect, as not to commit sin, and to be freed from evil thoughts and evil tempers.

29. Thus has the Lord fulfilled the things he spoke by his holy prophets, which have been since the world began; by Moses in particular, saying I "will circumcise thine heart, and the heart

of thy seed, to love the Lord thy God with all thy heart, and with all thy soul" (Deut. 30:6); by David, crying out, "Create in me a clean heart, and renew a right spirit within me" [Ps. 51:10]. And most remarkably by Ezekiel, in those words, "Then will I sprinkle clean water upon you, and you shall be clean; from all your filthiness, and from all your idols, will I cleanse you. A new heart also will I give you, and a new spirit will I put within you; and cause you to walk in my statutes, and you shall keep my judgments, and do them. You shall be my people, and I will be your God. I will also save you from all your uncleannesses. Thus says the Lord your God, in the day that I shall have cleansed you from all your iniquities, the heathen shall know that I the Lord build the ruined places; I the Lord have spoken it, and I will do it" (Ezek. 36:25, &c).

30. "Having therefore these promises, dearly beloved," both in the Law and in the Prophets, and having the prophetic word confirmed unto us in the Gospel, by our blessed Lord and his apostles; "let us cleanse ourselves from all filthiness of flesh and spirit, perfecting holiness in the fear of God" [2 Cor. 7:1]. "Let us fear, lest" so many "promises being made us of entering into his rest," which he that has entered into, has ceased from his own works, "any of us should come short of it" [Heb. 4:1]. "This one thing let us do, forgetting those things which are behind, and reaching forth unto those things which are before, let us press toward the mark, for the prize of the high calling of God in Christ Jesus" [Phil. 3:13–14]; crying unto him day and night, till we also are "delivered from the bondage of corruption, into the glorious liberty of the sons of God!" [Rom. 8:21].

The Promise of Sanctification

Ezekiel 36:25, &c

By the Rev. Mr. Charles Wesley

1 God of all power, and truth, and grace,
Which shall from age to age endure;
Whose word, when heaven and earth shall pass,
Remains, and stands for ever sure:

2 Calmly to thee my soul looks up,
And waits thy promises to prove;
The object of my steadfast hope,
The seal of thine eternal love.

3 That I thy mercy may proclaim,
That all mankind thy truth may see,
Hallow thy great and glorious name,
And perfect holiness in me.

4 Chose from the world, if now I stand
Adorned in righteousness divine;
If, brought unto the promised land,
I justly call the Savior mine;

5 Perform the work thou hast begun,
My inmost soul to thee convert;
Love me, forever, love thine own,
And sprinkle with thy blood my heart.

6 Thy sanctifying Spirit pour
To quench my thirst, and wash me clean;
Now, Father, let the gracious shower
Descend, and make me pure from sin.

7 Purge me from every sinful blot;
My idols all be cast aside.
Cleanse me from every evil thought,
From all the filth of self and pride.

8 Give me a new, a perfect heart,
From doubt, and fear, and sorrow free;
The mind which was in Christ impart,
And let my spirit cleave to thee.

9 O take this heart of stone away,
(Thy rule it doth not, cannot own);
In me no longer let it stay;
O take away this heart of stone.

10 The hatred of my carnal mind
Out of my flesh at once remove;
Give me a tender heart, resigned
And pure, and filled with faith and love.

11 Within me thy good Spirit place,
Spirit of health, and love, and power;
Plant in me thy victorious grace,
And sin shall never enter more.

12 Cause me to walk in Christ my way,
And I thy statutes shall fulfill;
In every point thy law obey,
And perfectly perform thy will.

13 Hast thou not said, who canst not lie,
That I your law shall keep and do?
Lord, I believe, though men deny.
They all are false, but thou art true.

14 O that I now, from sin released,
Thy word might to the utmost prove!
Enter into the promised rest,
The Canaan of thy perfect love!

15 There let me ever, ever dwell;
Be thou my God, and I will be
Thy servant: O set to thy seal;
Give me eternal life in thee.

16 From all remaining filth within,
Let me in thee salvation have;
From actual, and from inbred sin
My ransomed soul persist to save.

17 Wash out my old orig'nal stain;
Tell me no more it cannot be,
Demons or men! The Lamb was slain,
His blood was all poured out for me!

18 Sprinkle it, Jesu, on my heart!
One drop of thy all-cleansing blood
Shall make my sinfulness depart,
And fill me with the life of God.

19 Father, supply my every need;
Sustain the life thyself hast given;
Call for the corn, the living bread,
The manna that comes down from heaven.

20 The gracious fruits of righteousness,
Thy blessings unexhausted store,
In me abundantly increase,
Nor let me ever hunger more.

21 Let me no more in deep complaint
"My leanness, O my leanness!" cry;
Alone consumed with pining want,
Of all my Father's children I!

22 The painful thirst, the fond desire,
Thy joyous presence shall remove;
While my full soul does still require
Thy whole eternity of love.

23 Holy, and true, and righteous Lord,
I wait to prove your perfect will;
Be mindful of thy gracious word,
And stamp me with thy Spirit's seal!

24 Thy faithful mercies let me find,
In which thou causest me to trust;
Give me the meek and lowly mind,
And lay my spirit in the dust.

25 Show me how foul my heart hath been,
When all renewed by grace I am;
When thou hast emptied me of sin,
Show me the fullness of my shame.

26 Open my faith's interior eye,
Display thy glory from above,
And all I am shall sink and die,
Lost in astonishment and love.

27 Confound, o'erpower me with thy grace!
I would be by myself abhorred;
(All might, all majesty, all praise,
All glory be to Christ my Lord!)

28 Now let me gain perfection's height!
    Now let me into nothing fall!
Be less than nothing in thy sight,
And feel that Christ is all in all!

Appendix D

John Wesley's Sermon on The Scripture Way of Salvation[1]

"Ye are saved through faith."

—Eph. 2:8 KJV

Introduction

1. Nothing can be more intricate, complex, and hard to understand than religion, as it has been often described. And this is not only true concerning the religion of the heathens, even many of the wisest of them, but concerning the religion of those also who were, in some sense, Christians; indeed, and men of great name in the Christian world; men who seemed to be pillars thereof. Yet how easy to be understood, how plain and simple a thing, is the genuine religion of Jesus Christ; provided only that we take it in its native form, just as it is described in the oracles of God! It

is exactly suited, by the wise Creator and Governor of the world, to the weak understanding and narrow capacity of man in his present state. How observable is this, both with regard to the end it proposes, and the means to attain that end! The end is, in one word, salvation; the means to attain it, faith.

2. It is easily discerned, that these two little words, faith and salvation, include the substance of all the Bible, the marrow, as it were, of the whole Scripture. So much the more should we take all possible care to avoid all mistake concerning them, and to form a true and accurate judgment concerning both the one and the other.

3. Let us then seriously inquire, first, what is salvation? Secondly, what is that faith through which we are saved? Finally, how are we saved by faith?

I. What Is Salvation?

Salvation Is a Present Blessing

1. And, first, let us inquire: What is salvation? The salvation that is here spoken of is not what is frequently understood by that word, the going to heaven, eternal happiness. It is not the soul's going to Paradise, termed by our Lord, "Abraham's bosom." It is not a blessing which lies on the other side of death; or, as we usually speak, in the other world. The very words of the text itself put this beyond all question: "You *are* saved." It is not something at a distance: it is a present thing; a blessing of which, through the free mercy of God, you are now in possession. No, the words may be rendered, and that with equal propriety, "You have been saved"; so that the salvation which

is here spoken of might be extended to the entire work of God, from the first dawning of grace in the soul, till it is consummated in glory.

2. If we take this in its utmost extent, it will include all that is wrought in the soul by what is frequently termed "natural conscience," but more properly, "preventing grace"—all the drawings of the Father; the desires after God, which, if we yield to them, increase more and more—all that light by which the Son of God "enlightens everyone that comes into the world"; showing every man "to do justly, to love mercy, and to walk humbly with his God"—all the convictions which his Spirit, from time to time, works in every child of man; although it is true, the generality of men stifle them as soon as possible, and after a while forget, or at least deny, that they ever had them at all.

Salvation Includes Both Justification and Sanctification

3. But we are at present concerned only with that salvation which the apostle is directly speaking of. And this consists of two general parts, justification and sanctification.

Justification is another word for pardon. It is the forgiveness of all our sins; and, what is necessarily implied therein, our acceptance with God. The price whereby this has been procured for us (commonly termed "the meritorious cause of our justification"), is the blood and righteousness of Christ; or, to express it a little more clearly, all that Christ has done and suffered for us, till he "poured out his soul for the transgressors." The immediate effects of justification are, the peace of God, a "peace that passes all understanding," and a "rejoicing in hope of the glory of God" "with joy unspeakable and full of glory."

4. At the same time that we are justified, indeed, in that very moment, sanctification begins. In that instant we are born again, born from above, born of the Spirit: there is a *real* as well as a *relative* change. We are inwardly renewed by the power of God. We feel "the love of God shed abroad in our heart by the Holy Spirit which is given unto us"; producing love to all mankind, and more especially to the children of God; expelling the love of the world, the love of pleasure, of ease, of honor, of money, together with pride, anger, self-will, and every other evil temper; in a word, changing the earthly, sensual, devilish mind, into "the mind which was in Christ Jesus."

5. How naturally do those who experience such a change imagine that all sin is gone; that it is utterly rooted out of their heart, and has no more any place therein! How easily do they draw that inference, "I *feel* no sin; therefore, I *have* none: it does not stir; therefore it does not *exist*: it has no *motion*; therefore, it has no *being*!"

6. But it is seldom long before they are undeceived, finding sin was only suspended, not destroyed. Temptations return, and sin revives; showing it was but stunned before, not dead. They now feel two principles in themselves, plainly contrary to each other; "the flesh lusting against the Spirit"; nature opposing the grace of God. They cannot deny, that although they still feel power to believe in Christ, and to love God; and although his "Spirit [still] witnesses with their spirits, that they are children of God"; yet they feel in themselves sometimes pride or self-will, sometimes anger or unbelief. They find one or more of these frequently *stirring* in their heart, though not *conquering*; indeed,

perhaps, "thrusting sore at them that they may fall"; but the Lord is their help.

7. How exactly did Macarius, fourteen hundred years ago, describe the present experience of the children of God: "The unskillful," or inexperienced, "when grace operates, presently imagine they have no more sin. Whereas they that have discretion cannot deny, that even we who have the grace of God may be bothered again. For we have often had instances of some among the brethren, who have experienced such grace as to affirm that they had no sin in them; and yet, after all, when they thought themselves entirely freed from it, the corruption that lurked within was stirred up anew, and they were nearly burned up."

8. From the time of our being born again, the gradual work of sanctification takes place. We are enabled "by the Spirit" to "mortify the deeds of the body," of our evil nature; and as we are more and more dead to sin, we are more and more alive to God. We go on from grace to grace, while we are careful to "abstain from all appearance of evil," and are "zealous of good works," as we have opportunity, doing good to all men; while we walk in all his ordinances blameless, therein worshiping him in spirit and in truth; while we take up our cross, and deny ourselves every pleasure that does not lead us to God.

9. It is thus that we wait for entire sanctification; for a full salvation from all our sins, from pride, self-will, anger, unbelief; or, as the apostle expressed it, "go on to perfection." But what is perfection? The word has various senses: here it means perfect love. It is love excluding sin; love filling the heart, taking up the whole capacity of the soul. It is love "rejoicing evermore, praying without ceasing, in everything giving thanks."

II. What Is That Faith through Which We Are Saved?

But what is faith through which we are saved? This is the second point to be considered.

The Evidence and Conviction of Things Not Seen

1. Faith, in general, is defined by the apostle as ἔλεγχος πραγμάτων οὐ βλεπομένων (an evidence, a divine *evidence and conviction* (the word means both) *of things not seen*); not visible, not perceivable either by sight, or by any other of the external senses. It implies both a supernatural *evidence* of God, and of the things of God; a kind of spiritual *light* exhibited to the soul, and a supernatural *sight* or perception thereof. Accordingly, the Scripture speaks of God's giving sometimes light, sometimes a power of discerning it. So Saint Paul: "God, who commanded light to shine out of darkness, has shined in our hearts, to give us the light of the knowledge of the glory of God in the face of Jesus Christ." And elsewhere the same apostle spoke of "the eyes of our understanding being opened." By this two-fold operation of the Holy Spirit, having the eyes of our soul both *opened* and *enlightened*, we see the things which the natural "eye has not seen, neither the ear heard." We have a prospect of the invisible things of God; we see the *spiritual world*, which is all round about us, and yet no more discerned by our natural faculties than if it had no being. And we see the *eternal world*; piercing through the veil that hangs between time and eternity. Clouds and darkness then rest upon it no more, but we already see the glory that shall be revealed.

The Evidence and Conviction That Christ Loves Me

2. Taking the word in a more particular sense, faith is a divine *evidence* and *conviction* not only that "God was in Christ, reconciling the world unto himself," but also that Christ loved *me*, and gave himself for *me*. It is by this faith (whether we term it the *essence*, or rather a *property* thereof) that we *receive Christ*; that we receive him in all his offices, as our Prophet, Priest, and King. It is by this that he is "made of God unto us wisdom, and righteousness, and sanctification, and redemption."

3. "But is this the *faith of assurance*, or *faith of adherence*?" The Scripture mentions no such distinction. The apostle said, "There is one faith, and one hope of our calling"; one Christian, saving faith; "as there is one Lord," in whom we believe, and "one God and Father of us all." And it is certain, this faith necessarily implies an *assurance* (which is here only another word for *evidence*, it being hard to tell the difference between them) that Christ loved me, and gave himself for me. For "he that believes" with the true living faith "has the witness in himself": "the Spirit witnesses with his spirit that he is a child of God." "Because he is a son, God has sent forth the Spirit of his Son into his heart, crying, Abba, Father"; giving him an assurance that he is so, and a childlike confidence in him. But let it be observed, that, in the very nature of the thing, the assurance goes before the confidence. For a man cannot have a childlike confidence in God till he knows he is a child of God. Therefore, confidence, trust, reliance, adherence, or whatever else it be called, is not the first, as some have supposed, but the second branch or act of faith.

4. It is by this faith we are saved, justified, and sanctified; taking that word in its highest sense. But how are we justified and sanctified by faith? This is our third head of inquiry. And this being the main point in question, and a point of no ordinary importance, it will not be improper to give it a more distinct and particular consideration.

III. How Are We Saved by Faith?

Faith Is the Only Condition of Justification

1. First, how are we justified by faith? In what sense is this to be understood? I answer: Faith is the condition, and the only condition, of justification. It is the *condition*: none is justified but he that believes: without faith no man is justified. And it is the *only condition*: this alone is sufficient for justification. Everyone that believes is justified, whatever else he has or has not. In other words: no man is justified till he believes; every man when he believes is justified.

2. "But does not God command us to repent also? Indeed, and to 'bring forth fruits fit for repentance'; to cease, for instance, from doing evil, and learn to do well? And is not both the one and the other of the utmost necessity, so that if we willingly neglect either, we cannot reasonably expect to be justified at all? But if this be so, how can it be said that faith is the only condition of justification?"

God does undoubtedly command us both to repent, and to bring forth fruits fit for repentance; which if we willingly neglect, we cannot reasonably expect to be justified at all: therefore both repentance, and fruits fit for repentance, are, in some sense, necessary to justification. But they are not necessary in the *same sense* with faith, nor in the *same degree*. Not in the *same degree*; for those fruits are only necessary *conditionally*; if there be time and opportunity for them. Otherwise a man may be justified without them, as was the *thief* upon the cross (if we may call him so; for a late writer has discovered that he was no thief, but a very honest and respectable person!) but he cannot be justified without faith; this is impossible. Likewise, let a man have ever so much repentance, or ever so many of the fruits fit for repentance, yet all this does not at all avail; he is not justified till he believes. But the moment he believes, with or without those fruits, indeed, with more or less repentance, he is justified—not in the *same sense*; for repentance and its fruits are only *remotely* necessary, necessary in order for faith; whereas faith is *immediately* necessary to justification. It remains, that faith is the only condition, which is *immediately* and *proximately* necessary for justification.

Faith Is the Only Condition of Sanctification

3. "But do you believe we are sanctified by faith? We know you believe that we are justified by faith; but do not you believe, and accordingly teach, that we are sanctified by our works?" So it has been roundly and vehemently affirmed for these twenty-five years, but I have constantly declared just the contrary; and that in all manner of ways. I have continually testified in private and in public, that we are sanctified as well as justified by faith. And indeed the one of those great truths does exceedingly illustrate the other. Exactly as we are justified by faith, so are we sanctified by faith. Faith is the condition, and the only condition, of sanctification, exactly as it is of justification. It is the *condition*: none is sanctified but he that believes; without faith no man is sanctified.

And it is the *only condition*: this alone is sufficient for sanctification. Everyone that believes is sanctified, whatever else he has or has not. In other words, no man is sanctified till he believes: every man when he believes is sanctified.

4. "But is there not a repentance consequent upon, as well as a repentance previous to, justification? And is it not incumbent on all that are justified to be 'zealous of good works'? Indeed, are not these so necessary, that if a man willingly neglects them he cannot reasonably expect that he shall ever be sanctified in the full sense; that is, perfected in love? No, can he grow at all in grace, in the loving knowledge of our Lord Jesus Christ? Indeed, can he retain the grace that God has already given him? Can he continue in the faith that he has received, or in the favor of God? Do not you yourself allow all this, and continually assert it? But, if this be so, how can it be said that faith is the only condition of sanctification?"

5. I do allow all this, and continually maintain it as the truth of God. I allow that there is a repentance consequent upon, as well as a repentance previous to, justification. It is incumbent on all that are justified to be zealous of good works. And they are so necessary, that if a man willingly neglects them, he cannot reasonably expect that he shall ever be sanctified; he cannot grow in grace, in the image of God, the mind that was in Christ Jesus; no, he cannot retain the grace he has received; he cannot continue in faith, or in the favor of God. What is the inference we must draw from this? Why, that both repentance, rightly understood, and the practice of all good works—works of piety, as well as works of mercy (now properly so called, since they spring from faith)—are, in some sense, necessary to sanctification.

Repentance for Remaining Sin

6. I say, "repentance rightly understood," for this must not be confounded with the former repentance. The repentance consequent upon justification is widely different from that which is antecedent to it. This implies no guilt, no sense of condemnation, no consciousness of the wrath of God. It does not suppose any doubt of the favor of God, or any "fear that has torment." It is properly a conviction, wrought by the Holy Spirit, of the *sin* which still *remains* in our heart; of the *jronhma sarkos* (the carnal mind), which "does still *remain*" (as our Church speaks) "even in those that are regenerate"; although it does no longer *reign*; it has not now dominion over them. It is a conviction of our proneness to evil, of a heart bent to backsliding, of the still continuing tendency of the flesh to lust against the Spirit. Sometimes, unless we continually watch and pray, it lusts to pride, sometimes to anger, sometimes to love of the world, love of ease, love of honor, or love of pleasure more than of God. It is a conviction of the tendency of our heart to self-will, to atheism, or idolatry; and above all, to unbelief; whereby, in a thousand ways, and under a thousand pretenses, we are ever departing, more or less, from the living God.

7. With this conviction of the sin remaining in our hearts, there is joined a clear conviction of the sin remaining in our lives; still *cleaving* to all our words and actions. In the best of these we now discern a mixture of evil, either in the spirit, the matter, or the manner of them; something that could not endure the righteous judgment of God, were he extreme to mark what is done amiss. Where we least suspected it, we find a taint of pride or

self-will, of unbelief or idolatry; so that we are now more ashamed of our best duties than formerly of our worst sins: and hence we cannot but feel that these are so far from having anything meritorious in them, truly, so far from being able to stand in sight of the divine justice, that for those also we should be guilty before God, were it not for the blood of the covenant.

8. Experience shows that, together with this conviction of sin *remaining* in our hearts, and *cleaving* to all our words and actions; as well as the guilt which on account thereof we should incur, were we not continually sprinkled with the atoning blood; one thing more is implied in this repentance; namely, a conviction of our helplessness, of our utter inability to think one good thought, or to form one good desire; and much more to speak one word right, or to perform one good action, but through his free, almighty grace, first preventing us, and then accompanying us every moment.

The Fruit of Repentance

9. "But what good works are those, the practice of which you affirm to be necessary to sanctification?" First, all works of piety; such as public prayer, family prayer, and praying in our closet; receiving the supper of the Lord; searching the Scriptures, by hearing, reading, meditating; and using such a measure of fasting or abstinence as our bodily health allows.

10. Secondly, all works of mercy; whether they relate to the bodies or souls of men; such as feeding the hungry, clothing the naked, entertaining the stranger, visiting those that are in prison, or sick, or variously afflicted; such as the endeavoring to instruct the ignorant, to awaken the stupid sinner, to quicken

the lukewarm, to confirm the wavering, to comfort the feeble-minded, to succor the tempted, or contribute in any manner to the saving of souls from death. This is the repentance, and these the "fruits fit for repentance," which are necessary to full sanctification. This is the way in which God has appointed his children to wait for complete salvation.

11. Hence may appear the extreme mischievousness of that seemingly innocent opinion, that there is no sin in a believer; that all sin is destroyed, root and branch, the moment a man is justified. By totally preventing that repentance, it quite blocks up the way to sanctification. There is no place for repentance in him who believes there is no sin either in his life or heart: consequently, there is no place for his being perfected in love, to which that repentance is indispensably necessary.

12. Hence, it may likewise appear that there is no possible danger in *thus* expecting full salvation. For suppose we were mistaken, suppose no such blessing ever was or can be attained, yet we lose nothing: no, that very expectation quickens us in using all the talents which God has given us; indeed, in improving them all; so that when our Lord comes, he will receive his own with increase.

13. But to return. Though it be allowed, that both this repentance and its fruits are necessary to full salvation; yet they are not necessary either in the same sense with faith, or in the same degree. Not in the *same degree*; for these fruits are only necessary *conditionally*, if there be time and opportunity for them; otherwise a man may be sanctified without them. But he cannot be sanctified without faith. Likewise, let a man have ever so much of this repentance, or ever so many good works, yet all this does not at all avail: he is not sanctified till he believes. But the moment

he believes, with or without those fruits, indeed, with more or less of this repentance, he is sanctified. Not in the *same sense*; for this repentance and these fruits are only *remotely* necessary; necessary in order to the continuance of his faith, as well as the increase of it; whereas faith is *immediately* and *directly* necessary to sanctification. It remains, that faith is the only condition that is *immediately* and *proximately* necessary to sanctification.

God Is Able and Willing to Sanctify Us Now

14. "But what is that faith whereby we are sanctified; saved from sin, and perfected in love?" It is a divine evidence and conviction, first, that God has promised it in the Holy Scripture. Till we are thoroughly satisfied of this, there is no moving one step further. And one would imagine there needed not one word more to satisfy a reasonable man of this, than the ancient promise, "Then will I circumcise your heart, and the heart of your seed, to love the Lord your God with all your heart, and with all your soul, and with all your mind." How clearly does this express the being perfected in love; how strongly imply the being saved from all sin! For as long as love takes up the whole heart, what room is there for sin therein?

15. Secondly, it is a divine evidence and conviction that what God has promised he is able to perform. Admitting, therefore, that "with men it is impossible" to "bring a clean thing out of an unclean," to purify the heart from all sin, and to till it with all holiness; yet this creates no difficulty in the case, seeing "with God all things are possible." And surely no one ever imagined it was possible to any power less than that of the Almighty! But if

God speaks, it shall be done. God says, "Let there be light; and there is light"!

16. Thirdly, it is a divine evidence and conviction that he is able and willing to do it now. And why not? Is not a moment to him the same as a thousand years? He cannot want more time to accomplish whatever is his will. And he cannot want or stay for any more *worthiness* or *fitness* in the persons he is pleased to honor. We may therefore boldly say, at any point of time, "Now is the day of salvation!" "Today, if you will hear his voice, do not harden your hearts!" "Behold, all things are now ready; come unto the marriage!"

17. To this confidence, that God is both able and willing to sanctify us now, there needs to be added one thing more: a divine evidence and conviction that he does it. In that hour it is done: God says to the inmost soul, "According to your faith be it unto you!" Then the soul is pure from every spot of sin; it is clean "from all unrighteousness." The believer then experiences the deep meaning of those solemn words, "If we walk in the light as he is in the light, we have fellowship one with another, and the blood of Jesus Christ his Son cleanses us from all sin."

18. "But does God work this great work in the soul gradually or instantaneously?" Perhaps it may be gradually wrought in some; I mean in this sense, they do not advert to the particular moment in which sin ceases to be. But it is infinitely desirable, were it the will of God, that it should be done instantaneously; that the Lord should destroy sin "by the breath of his mouth," in a moment, in the twinkling of an eye. And so he generally does; a plain fact, of which there is evidence enough to satisfy any unprejudiced person. *You*, therefore, look for it every moment!

Look for it in the way above described; in all those *good works* to which you are "created anew in Christ Jesus." There in then no danger: you can be no worse, if you are no better, for that expectation. For were you to be disappointed of your hope, still you lose nothing. But you shall not be disappointed of your hope: it will come, and will not tarry. Look for it then every day, every hour, every moment! Why not this hour, this moment? Certainly you may look for it *now*, if you believe it is by faith.

And by this token you may surely know whether you seek it by faith or by works. If by works, you want something to be done *first, before* you are sanctified. You think, I must first *be* or *do* this or that. Then you are seeking it by works unto this day. If you seek it by faith, you may expect it as you are; and expect it now. It is of importance to observe, that there is an inseparable connection between these three points: expect it by faith; expect it *as you are*; and expect it *now*! To deny one of them, is to deny them all; to allow one, is to allow them all.

Do *you* believe we are sanctified by faith? Be true then to your principle; and look for this blessing just as you are, neither better nor worse; as a poor sinner that has still nothing to pay, nothing to plead, but "Christ *died*." And if you look for it as you are, then expect it *now*. Stay for nothing: why should you? Christ is ready; and he is all you want. He is waiting for you: he is at the door! Let your inmost soul cry out,

Come in, come in, thou heavenly Guest!
Nor hence again remove;
But sup with me, and let the feast
Be everlasting love.

Appendix E

Various Contemporary Denominations' Statements on Entire Sanctification

This section includes a handful of excerpts from a variety of denominations across the Wesleyan/Methodist family to help show the extent to which these traditions continue to affirm the importance of holiness and especially entire sanctification as a part of their identity and self-understanding. This list is not comprehensive. My hope is that a read through these statements will help people across the Methodist family, as I have broadly defined it in this book, to see how much they have in common with each other. I hope different denominations will see the way they are connected to a broader family of faith through our common connection to the gift of entire sanctification. I hope the benefit of seeing Methodism's most distinctive founding theological commitment affirmed in contemporary doctrinal statements offsets any omissions.

African Methodist Episcopal Church[1]

Catechism on Faith

Section IV.

Q. 1: How much is allowed by our brethren who differ from us, with regard to entire sanctification?

A. They grant, 1st. That every one must be entirely sanctified, in the article of death;

2d. That till then a believer daily grows in grace, comes nearer and nearer to perfection;

3d. That we ought to be continually pressing after this, and to exhort all others so to do.

Q. 3: What then is the point where-in we divide?

A. It is this: Whether we should expect to be saved from all sin, before the article of death?

Q. 6: Does the New Testament afford any further ground, for expecting to be saved from all sin?

A. Undoubtedly it does, both in those prayers and commands which are equivalent to the strongest assertions.

Q. 7: What prayers do you mean?

A. Prayers for entire sanctification; which, were there no such thing, would be mere mockery of God. Such in particular, are:

1. *Deliver us from evil*; or rather, *from the evil one*. Now when this is done, when we are delivered from all evil, there can be no sin remaining.
2. "*Neither pray I for these alone, but for them also which shall believe on me through their word: that they all may be one, as thou Father art in me and I in Thee, that they also may be*

one in us: I in them and thou in me, that they may be made perfect in one." (John 17:20–21, 23)

3. *I bow my knees unto the God and Father of our Lord Jesus Christ—that he would grant you—that ye being rooted and grounded in love, may be able to comprehend with all saints, what is the breadth and length and height; and to know the love of* Christ *which passeth knowledge, that ye might be filled with all the fulness of God.* (Eph. 3:14, 16, 19)
4. *The very God of Peace sanctify you wholly. And I pray God, your whole spirit, soul, and body, be preserved blameless unto the coming of our Lord* Jesus Christ. (1 Thess. 5:23)

Q. 8: What command is there to the same effect?

A. *Be ye therefore perfect as your Father which is in heaven is perfect.* (Matt. 5:48)

2. *Thou shalt love the Lord thy God with all thy heart, and with all thy soul, and with all thy mind.* (Matt. 22:37)

But if the love of God fill all the heart, there can be no sin there.

Q. 9: But how does it appear, that this is to be done before the article of death?

A. First, from the very nature of a command, which is not given to the dead, but to the living.

Therefore, *Thou shalt love the Lord thy God with all thy heart,* cannot mean, Thou shalt do this when you diest, but while thou livest.

Secondly, from express texts of scripture:

1. *The grace of God that bringeth salvation hath appeared to all men; teaching us, that having renounced ungodliness and wordly lusts, we should live soberly, righteously, and godly*

in this present world: looking for—the glorious appearing of our Lord Jesus Christ; *who gave himself for us, that he might redeem us from* all *iniquity; and purify unto himself a peculiar people, zealous of good works.* (Titus 2:11–14)

2. *He hath raised up a horn of salvation for us—to perform the mercy promised to our fathers; the oath which he swore to our father* Abraham, *that he would grant unto us, that we being delivered out of the hand of our enemies, should serve him without fear, in holiness and righteousness before him all the days of our life.* (Luke 1:69, 72–75)

Church of the Nazarene[2]

Articles of Faith

X. "Christian Holiness and Entire Sanctification"

We believe that sanctification is the work of God which transforms believers into the likeness of Christ. It is wrought by God's grace through the Holy Spirit in initial sanctification, or regeneration (simultaneous with justification), entire sanctification, and the continued perfecting work of the Holy Spirit culminating in glorification. In glorification we are fully conformed to the image of the Son.

We believe that entire sanctification is that act of God, subsequent to regeneration, by which believers are made free from original sin, or depravity, and brought into a state of entire devotement to God, and the holy obedience of love made perfect.

It is wrought by the baptism with or infilling of the Holy Spirit, and comprehends in one experience the cleansing of the heart from sin and the abiding, indwelling presence of the Holy Spirit, empowering the believer for life and service. Entire sanctification is provided by the blood of Jesus, is wrought instantaneously by grace through faith, preceded by entire consecration; and to this work and state of grace the Holy Spirit bears witness.

This experience is also known by various terms representing its different phases, such as "Christian perfection," "perfect love," "heart purity," "the baptism with or infilling of the Holy Spirit," "the fullness of the blessing," and "Christian holiness."

10.1

We believe that there is a marked distinction between a pure heart and a mature character. The former is obtained in an instant, the result of entire sanctification; the latter is the result of growth in grace.

We believe that the grace of entire sanctification includes the divine impulse to grow in grace as a Christlike disciple. However, this impulse must be consciously nurtured, and careful attention given to the requisites and processes of spiritual development and improvement in Christlikeness of character and personality. Without such purposeful endeavor, one's witness may be impaired and the grace itself frustrated and ultimately lost.

Participating in the means of grace, especially the fellowship, disciplines, and sacraments of the Church, believers grow in grace and in wholehearted love to God and neighbor.

Free Methodist Church[3]

Articles of Religion

SANCTIFICATION

¶119 Sanctification is that saving work of God beginning with new life in Christ whereby the Holy Spirit renews His people after the likeness of God, changing them through crisis and process, from one degree of glory to another, and conforming them to the image of Christ.

As believers surrender to God in faith and die to self through full consecration, the Holy Spirit fills them with love and purifies them from sin. This sanctifying relationship with God remedies the divided mind, redirects the heart to God, and empowers believers to please and serve God in their daily lives.

Thus, God sets His people free to love Him with all their heart, soul, mind, and strength, and to love their neighbor as themselves.

The United Methodist Church[5]

Of Sanctification

Sanctification is that renewal of our fallen nature by the Holy Ghost, received through faith in Jesus Christ, whose blood of atonement cleanseth from all sin; whereby we are not only delivered from the guilt of sin, but we are washed from its pollution, saved from its power, and are enabled, through grace, to love God with all our hearts and to walk in his holy commandments blameless.

The Confession of Faith of the Evangelical United Brethren Church[6]

Article XI—Sanctification and Christian Perfection

We believe sanctification is the work of God's grace through the Word and the Spirit, by which those who have been born again are cleansed from sin in their thoughts, words and acts, and are enabled to live in accordance with God's will, and to strive for holiness without which no one will see the Lord.

Entire sanctification is a state of perfect love, righteousness and true holiness which every regenerate believer may obtain by being delivered from the power of sin, by loving God with all the heart, soul, mind and strength, and by loving one's neighbor as one's self. Through faith in Jesus Christ this gracious gift may be received in this life both gradually and instantaneously, and should be sought earnestly by every child of God.

We believe this experience does not deliver us from the infirmities, ignorance, and mistakes common to man, nor from the possibilities of further sin. The Christian must continue on guard against spiritual pride and seek to gain victory over every temptation to sin. He must respond wholly to the will of God so that sin will lose its power over him; and the world, the flesh, and the devil are put under his feet. Thus he rules over these enemies with watchfulness through the power of the Holy Spirit.

The Salvation Army[4]

The Salvation Army has a doctrinal statement of eleven doctrines. The doctrine on full salvation, or entire sanctification, follows. They also have a *Handbook of Doctrine* that explains in much greater depth each of these eleven doctrines. This section includes the doctrine on full salvation and a brief excerpt from the much longer discussion of this doctrine in the *Handbook*.

On Full Salvation

We believe it is the privilege of all believers to be wholly sanctified, and that their whole spirit and soul and body may be preserved blameless unto the coming of our Lord Jesus Christ.

4. A RADICAL LIFE-CHANGE

God's sanctifying work is a life-changing experience whereby we are empowered to make radical changes of direction in our lives (2 Corinthians 5:14–15) so that the Spirit comes and lives his life in us (Galatians 2:20; Ephesians 3:14–19). Sometimes a compelling glimpse of the holiness of God opens our eyes to our need of purity. We may be stimulated to seek to live a holy life because we long for a more satisfying relationship with God. The call to service may lead to a deeper desire for sanctifying grace. We may experience the pain and agony of encountering evil and sin lurking within us. We may become aware of our inclination to give in to temptation or relax our guard. The Holy Spirit's leading and our own desire for more of God may in such circumstances lead to a spiritual crisis.

At such times the Holy Spirit is overwhelmingly present with power for holy living. We experience a moment of grace that leads to spiritual breakthrough. We move to a new level of relationship with the holy God, with others and with ourselves (Philippians 1:9–11).

Such life-changing moments are widespread, but dramatic experiences are not always a feature of our growth in holiness. The Holy Spirit deals with us as individuals and leads us into holiness in the way he sees fit.

We should judge the growth of our spiritual life by the quality of our obedience, and by a deepening and transforming commitment to love for God, other people and ourselves (Romans 12:1–2; Colossians 3: 5–14), rather than by the depth and intensity of our spiritual experiences.

The Wesleyan Church[7]

Articles of Religion

15. Sanctification: Initial, Progressive, Entire

236. We believe that sanctification is that work of the Holy Spirit by which the child of God is separated from sin unto God and is enabled to love God with all the heart and to walk in all His holy commandments blameless. Sanctification is initiated at the moment of justification and regeneration. From that moment there is a gradual or progressive sanctification as the believer walks with God and daily grows in grace and in a more perfect obedience to God. This prepares for the crisis of entire sanctification which is wrought instantaneously when believers present themselves as living sacrifices, holy and acceptable to God,

through faith in Jesus Christ, being effected by the baptism with the Holy Spirit who cleanses the heart from all inbred sin. The crisis of entire sanctification perfects the believer in love and empowers that person for effective service. It is followed by life-long growth in grace and the knowledge of our Lord and Savior, Jesus Christ. The life of holiness continues through faith in the sanctifying blood of Christ and evidences itself by loving obedience to God's revealed will.

Notes

Epigraph

1. John Wesley, Letter to Robert Carr Brackenbury, September 15, 1790, in *The Letters of John Wesley*, 8 vols., ed. John Telford (London: Epworth Press, 1931), 8:238.
2. R. W. Dale, *The Evangelical Revival* (London: Hodder and Stoughton, 1880), 39.

Prologue

1. John Wesley, from "A Plain Account of Christian Perfection," Section 25, in answer to Question 33, the last third of the answer.

Chapter One

1. John Wesley, Letter to Robert Carr Brackenbury, September 15, 1790, in *The Letters of John Wesley*, 8 vols., ed. John Telford (London: Epworth Press, 1931), 8:238.
2. The United Methodist Church may soon divide. Whether it does or not, I have the current church in mind as well as any new denominations that may arise. My argument is that the doctrine of entire sanctification is essential for Methodist vitality in all of its various expressions.
3. This section is an edited version of a post that was first published on my personal blog: https://kevinmwatson.com/2018/10/31/return/.
4. John Wesley, *A Plain Account of Christian Perfection as believed and taught by Mr. John Wesley from the year 1725 to the year 1777* (Franklin, TN: Seedbed, 2014), 42.

5. Vinson Synan, *The Holiness-Pentecostal Tradition: Charismatic Movements in the Twentieth Century* (Grand Rapids, MI: Eerdmans, 1997), xi. Donald W. Dayton has also demonstrated the Wesley roots of Pentecostalism in *The Theological Roots of Pentecostalism* (Grand Rapids: Baker Academic, 1987).
6. John Wesley, *Journal*, January 1, 1739, in *The Works of John Wesley*, vols. 18–24; *Journals and Diaries*, eds. W. Reginald Ward and Richard P. Heitzenrater (Nashville, TN: Abingdon, 1988–2003), 19:29 (italics mine).
7. For more information on the New Room Conference, check out: https://newroomconference.com.
8. For more information on Aldersgate, check out: https://aldersgateconference.org.
9. *The Book of Discipline of The United Methodist Church, 2016* (Nashville, TN: United Methodist Publishing House, 2016) ¶336, p. 270.

Chapter Two

1. John Wesley, "Thoughts upon Methodism," *Works of John Wesley*, vol. 9, *The Methodist Societies: History, Nature, and Design*, ed. Rupert E. Davies (Nashville, TN: Abingdon, 1989), 527 (italics mine).
2. John Wesley, Letter to George Merryweather, February 8, 1766, in *The Letters of John Wesley*, 8 vols., ed. John Telford (London: Epworth Press, 1931), 4:321 (emphasis original).
3 John Wesley, Letter to Robert Carr Brackenbury, September 15, 1790, in *The Letters of John Wesley*, 8 vols., ed. John Telford (London: Epworth Press, 1931), 8:238.
4. John Wesley, *A Plain Account of Christian Perfection as believed and taught by Mr. John Wesley from the year 1725 to the year 1777* (Franklin, TN: Seedbed, 2014), 113.
5. For more on the means of grace, see Andrew C. Thompson, *The Means of Grace: Traditioned Practice in Today's World* (Franklin, TN: Seedbed, 2015).
6. See Kevin M. Watson and Scott T. Kisker, *The Band Meeting: Rediscovering Relational Discipleship in Transformational Community* (Franklin, TN: Seedbed, 2017) and Kevin M. Watson, *Pursuing Social Holiness: The Band Meeting in Wesley's Thought and Popular Methodist Practice* (New York: Oxford University Press, 2014).
7. John Wesley, "Rules of the Band Societies," in *The Works of John Wesley*, vol. 9, *The Methodist Societies: History, Nature, and Design*, ed. Rupert E. Davies (Nashville, TN: Abingdon, 1989), 78. The full text of the "Rules of the Band Societies" can be found in appendix D.

8. John Wesley, *A Plain Account of Christian Perfection as believed and taught by Mr. John Wesley from the year 1725 to the year 1777* (Franklin, TN: Seedbed, 2014), 97.
9. John Wesley, Letter to Edward Jackson, January 6, 1781, in *The Letters of John Wesley*, 8 vols., ed. John Telford (London: Epworth Press, 1931), 7:47.
10. If you want to know more about my experience in bands and why I believe they are so important, see Kevin M. Watson and Scott T. Kisker, *The Band Meeting: Rediscovering Relational Discipleship in Transformational Community* (Franklin, TN: Seedbed, 2017), 14–16.
11. *The Book of Discipline of The United Methodist Church, 2016* (Nashville, TN: United Methodist Publishing House, 2016), ¶330, p. 258.
12. John Wesley, "The Nature, Design, and General Rules of the United Societies," in *Works* 9:69–73. See appendix A for the text of the "General Rules."
13. John Wesley, *Journal*, April 30, 1739, in Wesley *The Works of John Wesley*, vols. 18–24; *Journals and Diaries*, eds. W. Reginald Ward and Richard P. Heitzenrater (Nashville, TN: Abingdon, 1988–2003), 19:52–53.
14. Ibid., May 9, 1740, 19:149.

Chapter Three

1. Lawrence Coughlan, Letter to John Wesley, April 12, 1762, in *Arminian Magazine* 4:337–338. This account is cited in Kevin M. Watson, *Pursuing Social Holiness: The Band Meeting in Wesley's Thought and Popular Methodist Practice* (New York, Oxford University Press, 2014), 132.
2. John Fletcher, cited in *The Life and Journal of Mrs. Hester Ann Rogers*, ed. E. Davies (Boston Stereotype Foundry, 1882), 88–89.
3. Adam Clarke, Letter to John Wesley, 1784, in J. W. Etheridge, *The Life of the Rev. Adam Clarke, LL.D.* (New York: Carlton & Porter, 1859), 461–62.
4. Jarena Lee, *The Life and Religious Experiences of Jarena Lee, A Coloured Lady, Giving an Account of Her Call to Preach the Gospel, Revised and Corrected from the Original Manuscript, Written by Herself* (Philadelphia: Printed and Published for the Author, 1836). A critical edition of Lee's autobiography has been published in *Sisters of the Spirit: Three Black Women's Autobiographies of the Nineteenth Century*, ed. William L. Andrews (Bloomington, IN: Indiana University Press, 1986). The citations here are from the Andrews edition, 33. I discuss Jarena Lee in connection with the early American Methodist commitment to

holiness and entire sanctification in Kevin M. Watson, *Old or New School Methodism? The Fragmentation of a Theological Tradition* (New York: Oxford University Press, 2019), 38–40.

5. Phoebe Palmer, *Faith and Its Effects: Or, Fragments from My Portfolio* (New York: Joseph Longking, 1849), 72–73 (italics original).
6. F. G. Hibbard, *Biography of Rev. Leonidas L. Hamline, D.D., Late One of the Bishops of the Methodist Episcopal Church* (Cincinnati, OH: Hitchcock and Walden, 1880), 104–5.
7. Hester Ann Rogers, *Account of the Experience of Hester Ann Rogers; and Her Funeral Sermon, by Rev. T. Coke, LL.D. to Which Is Added Her Spiritual Letters* (New York: T. Mason and G. Lane, 1837), 100.
8. Joseph Benson, quoted in J. A. Wood, *Perfect Love; or, Plain Things for Those Who Need Them; Concerning the Doctrine, Experience, Profession, and Practice of Christian Holiness* (Philadelphia, PA: Samuel D. Burlock, 1861), 130.
9. Freeborn Garrettson, untitled, undated sermon on Luke 11:31, Garrettson Family Papers (box 1, folder 20). I discuss Garrettson at more length in *Old or New School Methodism?*, 42–43.
10. Jane Cooper, Letter to John Wesley, May 2, 1761, cited in John Wesley, *A Plain Account of Christian Perfection as believed and taught by Mr. John Wesley from the year 1725 to the year 1777* (Franklin, TN: Seedbed, 2014), 65–66.
11. John Ffirth, *Experienced and Gospel Labors of the Rev. Benjamin Abbott; to Which Is Annexed a Narrative of His Life and Death* (New York: Carlton & Phillips, 1853), 163. I cite this account in *Old or New School Methodism? The Fragmentation of a Theological Tradition* (New York: Oxford University Press, 2019), 44–45.
12. James Sigston, *Memoir of the Life and Ministry of Mr. William Bramwell, Lately an Itinerant Methodist Preacher* (New York: J. Emory and B. Waugh, 1830), 27.
13. Phoebe Palmer, *Pioneer Experiences: The Gift of Power Received by Faith* (New York: W. C. Palmer, Jr., 1872), 39–40.

Chapter Four

1. B. T. Roberts, "A Running Sketch" in *The Earnest Christian* IX, January 1865, 5–8.
2. For more on this story, see Kevin M. Watson, *Old or New School Methodism? The Fragmentation of a Theological Tradition* (New York: Oxford University Press, 2019).

3. I have written at length about one particular aspect of this story in Kevin M. Watson, *Old or New School Methodism? The Fragmentation of a Theological Tradition* (New York: Oxford University Press, 2019).
4. Melvin E. Dieter, *The Holiness Revival of the Nineteenth Century*, 2nd ed. (Lanham, MD: Scarecrow Press, 1996), 256.
5. Ibid.
6. Ibid.
7. Ibid.
8. These questions have been consistently asked in the United Methodist Church and can be found in *The Book of Discipline of The United Methodist Church, 2016* (Nashville, TN: United Methodist Publishing House, 2016), ¶336, 270.
9. Article XI, "Sanctification and Christian Perfection," *Book of Discipline of The United Methodist Church, 2016*. ¶104, p. 75.

Chapter Five

1. John Wesley, "The Principles of a Methodist Farther Explained," VI.4, in Wesley, *Works*, 9:227; John Wesley, "Thoughts upon Methodism," 18, in Wesley, *Works*, 9:529.
2. John Wesley, "The Scripture Way of Salvation," I.4, in *The Works of John Wesley*, vols. 1–4, *Sermons*, ed. Albert C. Outler (Nashville, TN: Abingdon, 1984–85), 2:158.
3. Ibid., III.14–17, 167–68.
4. Ibid., I.9, 160.
5. John Wesley, "Christian Perfection," II.14, in Wesley, *Sermons*, ed. Albert C. Outler (Nashville, TN: Abingdon, 1984–85), 2:112.
6. Ibid., II.20, 2:116.
7. Ibid., II.21, 2:117.
8. John Wesley, "Christian Perfection," II.24, in Wesley, *Sermons*, ed. Albert C. Outler (Nashville, TN: Abingdon, 1984–85), 2:118.
9. Ibid., II.25, 2:118.
10. Ibid., II.26, 2:119.
11. John Wesley, "Christian Perfection," II.27, in Wesley, *Sermons*, ed. Albert C. Outler (Nashville, TN: Abingdon, 1984–85), 2:119–120.
12. Ibid., II.28, 2:120.
13. John Wesley, "Scripture Way of Salvation," I.9, in Wesley, *Sermons*, ed. Albert C. Outler (Nashville, TN: Abingdon, 1984–85), 2:160, emphasis mine.

Chapter Six

1. John Wesley, "Christian Perfection" 2, in Wesley, *Sermons*, ed. Albert C. Outler (Nashville, TN: Abingdon, 1984–85), 2:99–100.
2. Ibid., 3, 2:100.
3. John Wesley, "Christian Perfection," I.1, in Wesley, *Sermons*, ed. Albert C. Outler (Nashville, TN: Abingdon, 1984–85), 2:100.
4. Ibid., 2:100–1.
5. Ibid., 2:101.
6. John Wesley, *Journal*, February 28, 1763, in *The Works of John Wesley*, vols. 18–24; *Journals and Diaries*, eds. W. Reginald Ward and Richard P. Heitzenrater (Nashville, TN: Abingdon, 1988–2003), 21:407.
7. John Wesley, "Christian Perfection," I.4, in Wesley, *Sermons*, ed. Albert C. Outler (Nashville, TN: Abingdon, 1984–85), 2:102.
8. John Wesley, "Christian Perfection," I.7, in Wesley, *Sermons*, ed. Albert C. Outler (Nashville, TN: Abingdon, 1984–85), 2:103.
9. John Wesley, "Christian Perfection," I.9, in Wesley, *Sermons*, ed. Albert C. Outler (Nashville, TN: Abingdon, 1984–85), 2:104.
10. Ibid., 2:105.

Chapter Seven

1. John Wesley, *A Plain Account of Christian Perfection as believed and taught by Mr. John Wesley from the year 1725 to the year 1777* (Franklin, TN: Seedbed Publishing, 2014), 3–4. The books mentioned here continue to be helpful guides to people who seek to pursue further study of Wesley's influences and Christian holiness. Three of these are available in new and easy-to-read editions published by Seedbed.
2. Wesley, *A Plain Account of Christian Perfection*, 4.
3. John Wesley, "Preface" in *Sermons on Several Occasions*, 5, in Wesley, *Sermons*, ed. Albert C. Outler (Nashville, TN: Abingdon, 1984–85), 1:105–6.
4. Ibid., 6, 1:106.
5. John Wesley, "The Principles of a Methodist Farther Explained," VI.4, in *The Works of John Wesley*, vols. 1–4, *Sermons*, ed. Albert C. Outler (Nashville, TN: Abingdon, 1984–85), 9:227.

Chapter Eight

1. I highly recommend starting a band meeting. God has used this particular group to change my life and the lives of many others

in miraculous ways. For an introduction to the band meeting and a guide to starting one, see Kevin M. Watson and Scott T. Kisker, *The Band Meeting: Rediscovering Relational Discipleship in Transformational Community* (Franklin, TN: Seedbed Publishing, 2017).

2. John Wesley, "The Scripture Way of Salvation" III.16, in Wesley, *Sermons*, ed. Albert C. Outler (Nashville, TN: Abingdon, 1984–85), 2:168, emphasis mine.
3. Ibid., III.14, 2:167.
4. Ibid., III.17, 2:168 (emphasis original).
5. John Wesley, "Scripture Way of Salvation" III.18, in Wesley, *Sermons*, ed. Albert C. Outler (Nashville, TN: Abingdon, 1984–85), 2:168–69, (emphasis original).
6. For an exceptional and accessible introduction to the means of grace, see Andrew C. Thompson, *The Means of Grace: Traditioned Practice in Today's World* (Franklin, TN: Seedbed Publishing, 2015).
7. For more on class and band meetings, see Kevin M. Watson, *The Class Meeting: Reclaiming a Forgotten (and Essential) Small Group Experience* (Franklin, TN: Seedbed Publishing, 2014) and Kevin M. Watson and Scott T. Kisker, *The Band Meeting: Rediscovering Relational Discipleship in Transformational Community* (Franklin, TN: Seedbed Publishing, 2017).

Appendix A

1. "The Nature, Design, and General Rules of the United Societies" in *The Book of Discipline of The United Methodist Church*, 2016 (Nashville, TN: United Methodist Publishing House, 2016), 77–80.

Appendix B

1. John Wesley, "Christian Perfection," in Wesley, *Sermons*, ed. Albert C. Outler (Nashville, TN: Abingdon, 1984–1985), 1:99–124. Language updated.

Appendix C

1. John Wesley, "The Scripture Way of Salvation," in *Making All Things New: Sermons on the Way of Salvation*, ed. Andrew C. Thompson (Franklin, TN: Seedbed Publishing, 2016), 13–28.

Appendix D

1. John Wesley, "Rules of the Band Societies," in *The Works of John Wesley*, vol. 9, *The Methodist Societies: History, Nature, and Design*, ed. Rupert E. Davies (Nashville, TN: Abingdon, 1989), 77–78.

Appendix E

1. *The Doctrines and Discipline of the African Methodist Episcopal Church* (Chapel Hill, NC: University of North Carolina Press, 2017), 30–33, emphasis original.
2. *Church of the Nazarene Manual, 2017–2021* (Kansas City, MO: Nazarene Publishing House, 2017), 31–32.
3. https://fmcusa.org/resources/fm-articles-of-religion.
4. https://www.salvationarmy.org/doctrine/handbookdoctrine PDF accessed March 20, 2020, 191, 193–94.
5. This article was added to the end of the UMC "Articles of Religion" at the 1939 merger that created the Methodist Church in 1939. The 1939 merger united the Methodist Episcopal Church, the Methodist Episcopal Church, South, and the Methodist Protestant Church. The article "Of Sanctification" came from the Methodist Protestant Church "Articles of Religion," *The Book of Discipline of The United Methodist Church, 2016* (Nashville, TN: United Methodist Publishing House, 2016), ¶104, p. 72.
6. The Confession of Faith of the Evangelical United Brethren Church became part of the doctrinal standards for The United Methodist Church at the 1968 merger of the Evangelical United Brethren and the Methodist Church that formed the UMC. *The Book of Discipline of The United Methodist Church, 2016* (Nashville, TN: United Methodist Publishing House, 2016), ¶104, p. 75.
7. *The Discipline of the Wesleyan Church, 2016* (Indianapolis, IN: Wesleyan Publishing House, 2016), 21.

More from Kevin M. Watson:

The Class Meeting

KEVIN M. WATSON

In *The Class Meeting*, Kevin Watson pulls a page from the playbook of John Wesley and brings it to life for today's Church. "Because most small groups are built around curricular study resources, people rarely get down to the real substance of what small groups are all about: transformation, or becoming like Christ. Most Christians know much more than they are practicing or applying to their lives. Class meetings were essential for the first Methodists, and they are essential today, because they helped people grow in faith in Christ and learn how to follow Jesus with their lives."

The Band Meeting

KEVIN M. WATSON AND SCOTT T. KISKER

The band meeting, a proven discipleship model for growing in love through the accountability of small, same-gender groups, was one of the defining characteristics of the Methodist movement started by John Wesley in the mid-1700s. In reflection on Wesley's class and band meeting structure, George Whitfield once said, "My brother Wesley acted wisely, the souls that were awakened under his ministry he joined in class, and thus preserved the fruits of his labor. This I neglected, and my people are a rope of sand." In *The Band Meeting*, Kevin Watson and Scott Kisker give an overview of the richness of this early tradition and introduce a practical approach for growing toward an authentic, transformation-oriented small group experience.

Available now at seedbed.com